ALL ROADS

LEAD

TO LOVE

CALEB'S AUTISM JOURNEY:

THE EARLY YEARS

Dr. Rhonda Brown-Crowder, Ph.D.

ALL ROADS LEAD TO LOVE

ISBN: 979-8-218—07582-8

Printed in the USA by Ingram Spark

DEDICATION

This book is dedicated to My Amazing Mother, Barbara Jean Brown. Thank You for teaching me how to pray and to understand the importance of doing so and maintaining a relationship with God. Thank You for laying a solid foundation of faith in me on which I stand today. Thank You for teaching me to be relentless, tenacious, and strong, to never accept 'No' for an answer, and to always find a way. Each of these things have caused me to be the strong, independent, self-sufficient woman I am today.

This book is dedicated to My Dearest Dad, Jessie Lee Brown. Thank You for always believing in me and loving me unconditionally. Thank You for always providing a strong shoulder to lean on and to cry, a listening ear, and an understanding heart. Thank You for your belief in Caleb and always reminding me that GOD has Great Things in store for him. Caleb Joshua Brown Crowder bears the responsibility of caring on your name. I will see to it that he does it proudly and honorably. You are forever in our hearts.

This book is dedicated to My Husband Curtis. Thank You for the love, grace, strength and support you gave me throughout my years of writing this book. You never once wavered in your belief in my ability to get this done. You are my greatest cheerleader! Thank You for loving our Son Caleb with the same fervor that I do, and for standing in Agreement with me that GOD has a Great Future planned for his life. Thank You for being a Great Father and Role Model for Caleb to follow. We Love You!

This book is dedicated to My Caleb Joshua Brown Crowder. The day you were born into this world became the Greatest Moment of my life. There is Nothing else in this world that could ever compare to you! For as long as I live, I will never fully understand why GOD chose to Bestow such Grace and Favor upon me, to make me Your Mother. It is a Role that I Humbly Accept and will Always Cherish.

You are my Greatest Treasure! I can't wait to see the things GOD has Planned for You!

TABLE OF CONTENTS

FOREWORD

If you have ever wondered if there are angels, you have only to look at Dr. Rhonda Brown-Crowder.

It is an honor of a lifetime to tell you about my dear friend, Dr. Brown-Crowder. She truly "walks the talk." In one of our early conversations regarding her precious son, I explained that she must be an advocate for him for the rest of her life. That is a huge task, but she looked at me with kind eyes and with steely determination and asked all the right questions to formulate a roadmap. At that moment, I understood, without a doubt, that I was in the presence of an exceptional human being. My love and respect for her and her sweet son have only grown since that very day.

The title of this book is significant in that we are called to understand that "All Roads Lead to Love," but at the same time we meet many angels along the way that help us grow. My favorite Administrator, Ms. Crumley, said that we are all linking arms to get up the hill. That visual gives a sense that none of us are left behind and none of us are running ahead. It is in the Community that we are stronger together. This is the idea behind the Gestalt Theory: the whole is more than the sum of its parts. With her tireless advocacy, Dr. Brown-Crowder has made us all more than the sum of our parts.

I know this book will make a difference in your life as we all face unknown roads and struggle with challenges. My prayer is that you find an angel as incredible as Dr. Rhonda Brown-Crowder. When you find that angel, hang on, your life will ever be different.

Jenetta C. Whitenight, M.A.Ed

PREFACE

"THE BEGINNING"

When I look at this picture, I imagine this new young mother and this adorable little boy having a conversation. She tells him that in a short amount of time he is going to be Diagnosed with Autism Spectrum Disorder and a Speech Impairment, and they are going to begin a lifelong Journey. She tells him while she is thrilled to finally have the Miracle Child it

took 2.5 years to conceive, she has no idea how to care for his Special Needs.

She tells him there will be days he will not be feeling well and will want to tell her, but he will find the words will not come. She tells him there will be days she will cry because she can't reach into his mind and understand how to help him. She tells him there will be times he will be frustrated and act out because he wants to communicate with her so badly, but his mind cannot fully comprehend how to do so.

She tells him there will be times when they are in public, people will stare and judge, and children will whisper and will look at him as if there was something wrong, and it is his fault. She tells him some of the people closest to them will turn their backs on them, while complete strangers will love him for life and celebrate his successes as their own.

She tells him she has no training or knowledge about the Roads and Paths they are about to take, but she will do everything she can to learn and to continue to educate herself. She tells him she will do everything within her power to make sure he lives a full and productive life, and he is exposed to all that life has to offer, like his Mainstream Peers. She tells him she will completely adjust her life, her thinking, her goals, and her expectations of him, to fit what he can do and not what others expect.

She tells him he will amaze her daily by excelling in the most incredible and sometimes unexpected ways. She tells him that despite his Autism and Speech Challenges, his amazing smile, his loving heart, and his energetic personality will always shine through. She tells him she will spend the rest of her life loving him, guiding him, teaching him, protecting him, fighting for him, and helping him, as GOD intended. She tells him that He is Truly Special and that His Life Matters...

She tells him they will travel many roads together in their lifetime. Some will be ultra-bright where they are shielding their eyes from the blinding light; some will be dimly lit and they can only see what's right in front of them; and some will be completely pitch black, where they are walking with their hands stretched out in front of them, trying to feel their way.

But, no matter what the circumstances, challenges, or triumph's they encounter, he must always remember that she will be with him, GOD will be with them, and All Roads Lead to Love...

ACKNOWLEDGMENTS

This Autism Journey is vast! There is no way the Roads we Special Needs Families must travel can be traversed alone. I believe GOD designed it that way; so, we can see how many amazing people HE has orchestrated to come into our lives when we need them the most.

The people mentioned have been an integral part of helping us carry the immense Autism Special Needs load and in meeting the responsibilities we are tasked with daily. I call them "Caleb's Community." There are more people than I can name for the space provided who have made such a difference in our lives. Here are some key ones.

Thank You to our current Grand Prairie Independent School District, Superintendent Linda Ellis, late Superintendent Dr. Susan Hull, former Executive Director of Special Education, Dorothea Gordon, all of Caleb's Amazing Teachers, Paraprofessionals, Administrators, Program Coordinators and Staff, for the support, input, guidance, and structure you've provided to help Caleb learn and grow and realize his potential.

Thank You to our Grand Prairie City Leaders, Mayor Ron Jensen, Former City Manager Tom Hart, Current City Manager and former Chief of Police, Steve Dye, Chief of Police Daniel Scesney, Retired Parks Director Rick Herold, and so many others who have embraced our Special Needs Community wholeheartedly and continue to promote innovative strategies for inclusion, support, and services for our unique population and families.

Thank You to Caleb's former Paraprofessionals Marshae Griggs and Jennifer Rosales for being my beta readers for this book project. Your input was invaluable! Thank You both also for supplying such love and support for Caleb in the classroom, and for maintaining that connection beyond it. Thank You for believing in Caleb. He loves you both so much!

Thank You to Tonya Brown of *TCB Professional Editing Services* for providing your expertise to this body of work, and for helping me to produce the best product possible.

Thank You to Caleb's late Dear Teacher Kathleen Wallis for your infectious enthusiasm for working with Caleb; for your unending belief in his ability to learn; and for your unrelenting love, friendship, and support for me as a Parent. We Miss You Deeply. We will always treasure your memory. You are forever in our hearts.

Thank You to these Awesome Grand Prairie ISD Special Education Employees Caleb and I met during his first summer camp right after his Diagnosis: Norma, Amanda, Jennifer, Lynn, Bud, Stephanie, Andrea, Jackie, Celina, and Tracie. You all were our first introduction to GPISD's Special Education Program. You were warm, friendly, kind, and welcoming, and you made the scariest time of our lives more bearable. Thank You for making both Caleb and I feel loved, valued, and accepted. You each have had the pleasure of watching Caleb grow up throughout the years and have watched him do great things. Both he and I will always have a special place in our hearts for you. May you continue to do your wonderful work of blessing our Special Needs Children and their families. We Love You!

I sincerely appreciate each person acknowledged here! Thank You for the contributions you have made in my life, Caleb's life, and to our family!

In Loving Memory of Caleb's Teacher: Kathleen Norris Wallis

I had the privilege of sharing a few words at Caleb's Teacher, Dear Kathleen's Service, as a Student Parent and Friend. These are some of the heartfelt words that I shared...

When the Pandemic happened, I was petrified at the thought of my Caleb having to do online learning, all while having a new teacher he had never met before. As the Parent of an Autistic Child, the one thing I worried about the most was his potential loss of learning.

In October of last year, I got my first glimpse as to the kind of Person and Teacher Kathleen was, and how committed she was to her students. When I opened my mailbox one day, there was a large envelope in there addressed to Caleb from her. We opened it and saw she had sent him a Fun Arts and Crafts project to do for Halloween. She had sent these to all her students. In the time of COVID Chaos, Calamity, and Uncertainty, receiving that package from Kathleen felt like she was Shining a Light of Hope into the Darkness.

I loved Kathleen's Excitement for Caleb's learning, and her Genuine Belief that he could do so. Very few people can match my belief in Caleb's ability and potential, but Kathleen did! *She did all of this while battling cancer...* You would never have known what she was going through because she gave all of herself in whatever moment she was in. She was always thinking of others, more than herself.

Kathleen exhibited the epitome of Joy and Enthusiasm while working with our Special Needs Students. She loved it So Much! Our Students KNEW she loved them, and she wanted the best for them.

She was not only Caleb's Teacher, but she became my Dearest Friend

I miss her deeply... She is forever in our hearts...

A WORD FROM THE AUTHOR

I am writing this book from the beginning of Caleb receiving his Autism Spectrum Disorder and Speech Impairment Diagnosis. I wanted to share the processes and pitfalls we experienced as we began this Special Needs Journey.

Firstly, I wrote this book to educate those who are not raising a child with Autism or other Special Needs to highlight our day-to-day challenges in raising our children. I wanted to provide valuable insight on things you can do to make the enormous load we carry a bit lighter.

Secondly, I wrote this book for those who have been on this Journey for a while, raising a child with Autism or other Special Needs. I wanted you to know that I deeply understand your hopes, fears, challenges, and triumphs; and to remind you that you are not alone.

Finally, I wrote this book for those parents who just received your Special Needs Child's Diagnosis and are at the beginning of this Journey. It is my intention to share with you knowledge and helpful strategies I learned throughout the years. I hope it provides you with a greater sense of direction and will help make your lives easier.

I was working on my Ph.D. when Caleb received his Autism Spectrum Disorder and Speech Impairment Diagnosis. You can imagine the level of stress and pressure I was under trying to educate myself on a Disorder that was completely foreign to me. I was doing this while trying to meet my educational demands and raising this little boy with his unique needs. By GOD'S Grace I was able to get through it! I share this information with you because I want you to know, no matter what mountains you are trying to climb and things you want to accomplish while raising your Special Needs Child, it can be done!

It has been a beautiful, brightly colorful picture, watching My Caleb's story unfold from his initial Diagnosis until now! He has far exceeded my expectations! As the title of this book states, *"All Roads Lead to Love,"* I have found this to be true. The remarkable thing is, while I often thought and expected us to travel those roads in a certain way, Caleb had an entirely different idea. It's been interesting and fun traveling through life with him, seeing things through his eyes. I don't claim to be an expert on all children with Autism or Special Needs, but I am an expert on Caleb and his Journey. So, I write and share my experiences and knowledge as an expert from that perspective.

Forgive me, my fellow Special Needs Parents of those who are also raising a child with Autism, if my terminology does not match yours. I fully understand the "appropriate" phrases to use to describe those with Autism versus those who do not have it are: neurotypical and neurodivergent.

In this book I chose to use the term "Mainstream" for those who are neurotypical to differentiate between those who have Autism and those who do not. I felt this was the best way to simplify my message so everyone could understand it whether they are raising someone on the Autism Spectrum or not. You might feel completely different about my choices, and that's okay. I encourage you to use whatever terms you feel best fits your child's truth.

While Caleb is older now, I wanted to start from the beginning of his Autism and Speech Impairment Diagnosis, so you could see the triumphs, downfalls, and the hopes and despair of a parent trying to figure out how to navigate through it all. I wanted you to walk through the years with me: the unending meetings, the collection of therapies, the pain of hearing all the *"he will never's"* and *"he can't's,"* and the relentless search to discover my son's personal "truth" to better prepare him for this world. I wanted to allow you to walk a bit of the distance with us on this arduous, unpredictable, amazingly beautiful Journey.

For those of you who are raising a child with Autism or other Special Needs, it is my hope that as you go on this Journey with Caleb and I and read about his early years, you will be inspired, strengthened, and renewed with hope for your child's future.

For those of you who are not raising a child with Autism or other Special Needs, it is my hope that your life's perspective will completely change, and you will seek out ways to be more helpful and supportive to those who are raising a Special Needs Child. It is my hope that you will hold their hand when they cry, even if you don't understand their pain; and you will shout with joy and celebrate with them, even if you don't understand the occasion.

Before I finish, please know that while I am clearly familiar with the Rules of Grammar, and understand being grammatically correct is important, I wrote this book based on the way I hear things in my heart. Consequently, you will find that on occasion, in order for me to adequately express my thoughts, the two do not always align.

This book is the beginning of Caleb's *"All Roads Lead to Love"* Series. I am currently working on Book 2, *"Caleb's Autism Diagnosis: The Transition Years,"* which will be coming soon!

I am honored to share our story with you.

CHAPTER ONE
"THE DEFINING MOMENT"

Years ago, when Caleb was around five years old and had recently been diagnosed with Autism, I decided to make an unexpected stop at Walgreens to pick up a few items. I had just picked Caleb up from the Babysitter. Normally, when I wanted to go out and get something, I usually waited until my husband Curtis was home so I could leave Caleb with him and go alone. In most cases it was easier and faster for me to do it this way.

However, on that day I knew I only needed to pick up a few items, so I decided to make a quick stop.

As we were walking towards the store, instead of holding my hand, Caleb wrapped his arms around my waist, buried his head next to me, and closed his eyes. I wrapped my arms around him to reassure him that I was there with him and that everything was okay. As he squeezed his eyes shut, I noticed the little dimple in his left cheek that only appears when he does certain things. I told him to open his eyes so he could see where he was going. And, like always, he did just that. He still held on tightly to me, however.

When we entered the store, everything was fine. Caleb didn't seem to have any apprehension, as he sometimes does when we first go

2

into a store. He had released his hold on my waist and was now holding my hand. As we were walking around and I was looking for my items, I suddenly started feeling Caleb pulling a bit against my hand. Instead of walking with me and keeping up, he started pulling away from me even more. His body became tense, and I could sense he was starting to feel anxious. I held on to his hand and continued shopping, hoping that it would pass. At the same time, in the back of my mind I started questioning my decision to stop by the store, rather than waiting until later when I could come alone. The last thing I wanted was for Caleb to get upset and have a meltdown in the store.

Suddenly, Caleb stopped. He looked scared and confused, like he didn't know where he was. He even looked at me like he didn't know who I was. This all happened in a matter of seconds. I tried to console him and tell him everything was okay, and that mommy was there. It seemed the more I tried to console him, the more anxious he became. I tried to grab his hand to reassure him, but he pulled away from me. He wouldn't let me touch him. I was trying to get him next to me so I could help him become centered again and know he was not alone. Not only was he out of my reach and wouldn't let me touch him, but he then began to cry. The greatest feeling of helplessness came over me. I didn't know what to do. As a mother, I wanted to console my child and reassure him that everything was okay, but he wouldn't let me.

People in the store started looking at us trying to figure out what was 'wrong' with my child. It was in that moment that my whole life changed. My view of Caleb dealing with Autism, changed. Up until then, I was always concerned about what people would think when they knew Caleb had Autism, how they would respond to him, and even to me. In that moment, I suddenly decided it didn't matter what people thought about my son and the fact that he dealt with Autism. My desire to try to minimize his Diagnosis in the eyes of other people suddenly became irrelevant. In that moment, all I wanted to do was to reconnect with Caleb to take away his fear, and to let him know that he was not alone.

Instead of standing over him trying to get his attention, I instinctively got down on my knees in the middle of the store aisle. I got down on his level where I knew he could see me. I looked him in the eyes and held out my hand for him to come to me. I used my words to soothe him and to let him know it was okay. Everything in me wanted to just go and grab Caleb and hold him until he felt it was safe enough to come back into that present moment. But I knew I had to restrain myself from doing so because it would only make things worse and him more afraid. I had to wait for him to come to me.

Gradually, I could see a sense of calm come over Caleb. He seemed fully aware and present again in the moment, and in his recognition of me as his mommy. In what seemed like an eternity, he finally walked over to me, slowly and hesitantly, and eventually took my hand. I stayed on that floor talking to Caleb, holding his hand and consoling him, until his beautiful smile re-appeared. At that moment, I knew he was okay again. I didn't care who was watching or what people were saying about my son or me. My only goal was to make sure Caleb knew he was safe and okay, and that I was right there with him.

In that moment, it was as if the whole world had disappeared. The shoppers disappeared. The products on the store shelves disappeared. The walls disappeared; and all that was left was Caleb and me. My heart was so sad and broken to see the look of fear on Caleb's face. I was determined to do whatever I could to help him through that moment, which was obviously so frightening for him.

Even though he seemed to be okay, I went ahead and quickly finished my shopping and left. Sharing that moment with Caleb really touched me to my soul. I already knew that GOD had given me a great responsibility in taking care of my son, (as he's dealing with his Special Needs), but The Lord helped me to see things on an even deeper level. I realized, to Caleb I am his whole world. I am his safety net. I am the one person he can come to for comfort when he is afraid. I am his center and his gauge for knowing that everything will be okay.

It was in that moment that The Lord helped me to also realize that Caleb was my sole responsibility. If I had not been there, Caleb would have thought he was all alone in this big, sometimes cruel, world. The thought of him feeling that way was heartbreaking. Knowing how scary this world can be for a Mainstream Child, I understood how much greater it can be for our children with Special Needs. In that moment, I was also reminded again of the depth of the responsibility GOD had given me to take care of this child and to raise him to navigate in this world.

GOD knew HE couldn't trust giving Caleb to just any parents, as he is dealing with his Special Needs. HE had to make sure HE gave Caleb to the right parents. If you would've asked me before I had Caleb if I was 'that' parent, I would have told you 'No way!' For a long time, because of my upbringing, I didn't even want to have children because I always questioned my ability to be a good mother; and, yet GOD gave me one of HIS most special and prized possessions to take care of while here on this earth. HE obviously saw something in me that I didn't see in myself.

Now that I am Caleb's mother, I have come to realize every day that there are qualities that GOD placed in me that I never knew were there before. These qualities enable me to have the patience, hope, fortitude, tenacity, motivation, drive, and faith to do the things that Caleb requires daily. It is my job to prepare him to the best of my ability to live in this world. It is one thing to raise a Mainstream Child and teach them the ways of the world, but it is an entirely different challenge to teach your child with Special Needs how to function independently in this world; especially when their communication is limited through speech, or they are nonverbal.

I realize one of my purposes in life is to be a Servant to Caleb. GOD gave me someone who would need assistance in doing many of the routine things in life, not once, not twice, but over and over again, day after day. I never imagined I would ever have the patience to function in such a role! And yet, just when I feel I have reached the point where I am breaking and cannot take anymore, GOD allows me to see Caleb through HIS Eyes. And suddenly I find myself overcome with love and compassion and tenderness, and all I want to do is help him, care for him, and do all I can to make life easier and better for him. It has become abundantly clear to me that Caleb is here for me, and I am here for him, and we are the Perfect Pair to walk this Autism Journey called life, together.

CHAPTER TWO
"WHERE DID MY BABY BOY GO?"

Before, I got married, I told my husband Curtis I didn't want to have children, but I wanted to reserve the right to change my mind. Fortunately, he agreed. I wanted to make sure I entered the marriage being transparent with a clear set of expectations. It wasn't that I didn't like children, but I always questioned my ability to be a good mother and to be able to relate to children, based on my upbringing. I guess I didn't want to 'mess up' in raising them. Five years into the marriage I had a complete change of heart, and decided I wanted to be a mother. I believe it was GOD who put that desire in my heart. One day I was okay with not having children, and the next it was all I could think about.

Due to my complex medical history and previous multiple surgeries, my doctor all but told me I should abandon the idea of conceiving, give up on having children myself, and adopt. While I am not against adoption, that was not something I wanted to do. He also suggested I have a fourth surgery and procedure to see if it would improve my odds of getting pregnant. The process was going to be very intense and did not guarantee I would have a greater chance of conceiving.

After giving it some thought, I decided I was not going to have any more surgeries nor take any more unknown drugs. I had reached my limit of trying to conceive and told GOD if HE wanted me to have a child, HE would have to bless me with one. HE spoke to me and told me I would conceive Caleb Joshua Crowder and he was going to do great things. Two-and-one–half years later, I became pregnant with Caleb. The strange thing was, due to my earlier medical condition, I didn't even know I was pregnant with him until almost four months later!

I was feeling a little odd, and out of the blue my husband Curtis suggested that I take a pregnancy test. Sure enough, it came back positive! We were both stunned! I took three more tests just to be sure! When the doctor sent us in for a sonogram to confirm the pregnancy, the nurse, thinking I was only a few weeks along, warned we probably weren't going to be able to see much. You can imagine our utter shock and surprise when she put the wand on my stomach and a nearly 4-month-old baby popped up on the screen sucking its thumb! I almost fell off the table! Curtis and I both pointed at the screen and said, 'There's a Baby in there!" It was Hilarious! Needless to say, it was a huge shock and a very scary and exciting time. Suddenly, we went from wanting to have a baby for the past 2.5 years, to needing to prepare for his arrival within 5 months!

Caleb was born early at 38 weeks during a scheduled C-section birth. My pregnancy was so high risk, and my health so fragile, the doctors didn't want to risk me going into labor, so they scheduled his delivery. After he was born, while he was a little slow in meeting some of his milestones, Caleb was developing 'normally' as a Mainstream, Neurotypical Child. He was saying words very early, and we were proudly convinced he was a "Baby Genius". At age one, we even bought the *"Your Baby Can Read Program"* to help him to develop his vocabulary even more. Life was good!

When Caleb went in for his 18-month vaccinations, it seemed as routine as all the other appointments except this time he got really sick afterwards. He threw up for the first time ever in his life, and he ran a fever. None of these things had ever happened when he received his earlier vaccinations. From that moment forward, things began to quickly change for our son, and his development deteriorated right before our eyes.

There are two main arguments in the Autism World about vaccinations. Some believe the vaccinations our children receive at the 18-month mark causes Autism; others believe they have nothing to do with causing it, and this is just the developmental period where if a child has Autism, or a genetic disposition to it, it is more likely to start manifesting itself at this stage. I had no idea about any of those things. I just knew that Caleb was suddenly not the same.

The little boy who used to love saying words without prompting, enjoyed listening to music and dancing, and was able to go into loud public places with ease, suddenly started regressing. Eventually, he was saying fewer words until he was using gestures more than words to communicate.

Caleb started becoming very sensitive to loud noises and light, and he started screaming and crying uncontrollably when going into loud public places. We had no idea what was going on with him.

Our main concern was the regression of Caleb's language. He went from speaking several words and repeating everything you told him to say, to saying virtually nothing at all. Because he was our only child, and most of our friends' children were older, we had no direct point of reference to measure Caleb's developmental progress. Yes, there were formal developmental guidelines, but so many people told us stories about how they talked later in life or someone they knew started talking late; so, we equated Caleb's delay to that reason. His pediatrician was aware of his delays but not overly concerned. I now realized he was not very knowledgeable on the subject at that time. Autism never entered any of our minds. We had no idea what it was.

When Caleb was about 3.5 years old, I saw a commercial on TV that was talking about Autism. It showed a little boy who was at a birthday party. While all the other little children were sitting together around the birthday table, this little boy was sitting off by himself, playing alone. He was apart from the group playing in his own world. He seemed totally oblivious to the things that were going on around him. As I watched the commercial, I got a sick feeling in the pit of my stomach. While Caleb didn't exhibit all of the behaviors they were describing: he didn't mind being touched, he was very loving, affectionate, outgoing, and made great eye contact; the scene with the child playing alone hit home. I saw my son in that moment.

The last thing in the world I wanted to believe was Caleb had Autism. I felt there was no way I would be able to have the skills or the know-how to be able to raise a Special Needs Child. I started doing some research on the subject. The more I learned about the Disorder, the more things started to line up concerning Caleb. I was so afraid of the fact that this might be what my son was dealing with, I refused to even say the word out loud. I couldn't even bring up the subject with my husband Curtis at that time. I just kept my fears to myself and hoped they weren't true.

In time, we did at least start the discussion that this might be what was going on with Caleb. I learned Curtis had the same fears but was afraid to share them. It was the most difficult and scariest discussion we had ever had as a married couple. We agreed, despite our fears, we had to pursue the matter further to see what was going on with Caleb and to get him the best help possible.

When Caleb was almost 4 years old, we decided to have him evaluated through the Early Childhood Intervention Program in our School District. There were five Certified Specialists involved: Speech, Occupational Therapy, Diagnostician, School Counselor, and School Nurse. Each of them tested Caleb in their areas of expertise, and after about three weeks, the Diagnosis was given: Caleb had Autism Spectrum Disorder and a Speech Impairment.

I was in a state of shock when the School Counselor met with me privately to discuss the results. She kept asking me if I had any questions-waiting for me to react outwardly, I guess. I just sat there in a state of shock and said 'No.' I suppose most mothers probably cried at the news. I felt numb and in a daze. I wouldn't allow myself to feel anything. I was afraid if I gave into my emotions and went down that road, it might be a long time before I came back. I had already told myself before the meeting, no matter what the Diagnosis was, (I already suspected it would be Autism), that I was going to focus on *what I could do* to solve the problem and not *what caused* the problem.

I realize now, this reaction was a form of denial in a sense, but that was the only way I could deal with the news at that time. I took all the pamphlets she gave me on recommended services, and his 32-page written Diagnosis report, and left. I didn't shed a tear. In my mind, shedding a tear would represent my giving into a fate of hopelessness and defeat for Caleb's future. It would be admitting the Diagnosis was final, and something he couldn't overcome.

For a long time, I didn't tell anyone about Caleb's Diagnosis, besides my husband Curtis. I especially didn't tell my friends and family because I didn't want them to judge Caleb and think less of him. I didn't want them to reject him and stop loving him because of his Diagnosis. I didn't want them to ostracize him and treat him as if he were flawed.

Even a year after Caleb's Diagnosis, I still couldn't bring myself to even say the word – *Autism* aloud. I experienced a lot of guilt and shame. I asked myself repeatedly what I might have done to cause his Diagnosis. Was it because of my earlier health issues? Was it because I didn't know I was pregnant during his first trimester and didn't receive proper care? Was it because of something I did or didn't do? I wondered what people would think. Would they think less of My Caleb as a person? Would they blame me? Would other children bully him? It was a very dark time for me. I now realize it was necessary, however, for me to go through it as part of my process for healing and acceptance.

Within a week of Caleb's Diagnosis, an ARD (Admission Review Dismissal) Meeting was held at his school to have him formally start Pre-K in a PPCD (Preschool Programs for Children with Disabilities) CARE (Children with Autism and Related Exceptionalities) Program. The meeting was held the week before Thanksgiving Break. Caleb starteddon't kick usschool the following Monday after the holiday, one week after his 4th Birthday.

Not only did I have to deal with the most devastating Diagnosis about my son, but I also had to deal with the fact that for the first time ever in our lives, we would be separated from each other for hours during the day. Up until that point, Caleb and I had always been together. I felt like our whole world was falling apart. We both went through a lot of separation anxiety. Not only did I miss him terribly, but I was also so afraid I wasn't going to be able to handle all the things that went with raising a child with Special Needs. I thought I was going to crumble and let Caleb down.

After Caleb's Diagnosis, I went through a time of mourning. While my son was not deceased, a part of me mourned for the son that I gave birth to: the one whom I had so many high hopes and dreams for his future; the one whom I loved hearing his sweet, little voice talking to me and repeating words; the one whom I saw possibly one day becoming a doctor, just like his mother; and all of the countless other hopes and dreams I imagined for his future. For a little while, the child that I gave birth to was lost to me, and I had no idea what the future held for the one who had received this Diagnosis.

I was afraid for Caleb's future. I wondered what would become of him, and how he would get along in this big, and sometimes cruel, world. I wondered what kind of life my son would have. Would he be able to one day marry and have children? Would he be able to work and have a career? Would he be able to one day live on his own? How would he manage if something happened to me or his father? Would his Autism Diagnosis be permanent? Would there ever be a cure?

13

As sad and lost as I felt during that time, I knew that I had to find a way to deal with what happened and to move on, for Caleb's sake. I knew I couldn't stay stuck on the Diagnosis and what the doctors and specialists, and everyone else were telling me about my son's bleak future. I knew that no matter how hard it was for me to deal with this change, I had to find a way to put my own feelings aside and focus on making sure Caleb had the best chance possible in life, even under the most challenging circumstances.

It would have been easy for me to focus on '*why*' this happened to Caleb and if the vaccination caused it. I had people asking me which side of the argument I fell on about vaccinations and Autism. The more they talked about it, the angrier and more helpless I felt. I came to realize, dwelling on the '*why*' and even answering the question was not in any way going to help Caleb. So, I decided I would spend all of my energy focusing on *what* I could do to help Caleb from that point forward, to better his future, rather than focusing on the past and what might have caused his condition.

Making that decision was the best thing I could have ever done. It gave me back the sense of control I needed, to know that I could do something to make things better for Caleb's future. And it took away that overwhelming feeling of helplessness and despair that my son's future was doomed and already decided. From that moment forward, I drew my strength from knowing the more I educated myself on services that were available for Caleb and found ways I could better prepare and equip him for his future, the more at peace I became in dealing with the situation.

I realized while Caleb had this Autism Diagnosis, it was still possible to work within the confines of the Diagnosis to find the right 'formula' of learning and life for him. I knew if we could find that right method or formula of learning for him, he would have the ability to learn and grow just like his Mainstream Peers. While his learning and development would require more time, adaptations, accommodations, and resources, it was something that could be done.

For someone like me who has very high expectations of myself, and in the beginning for my son, it was a hard reality to accept the fact that his accomplishments would come much later and much slower than I had hoped or imagined. But, as time progressed, I realized this was the beauty of this Precious Autism Journey GOD ordained for Caleb and me to take together. His Diagnosis forced me to stop and recognize every bit of progress he made, and to celebrate every success. These are moments I likely would have otherwise overlooked under normal circumstances.

.

CHAPTER THREE
"PARALLEL UNIVERSES"

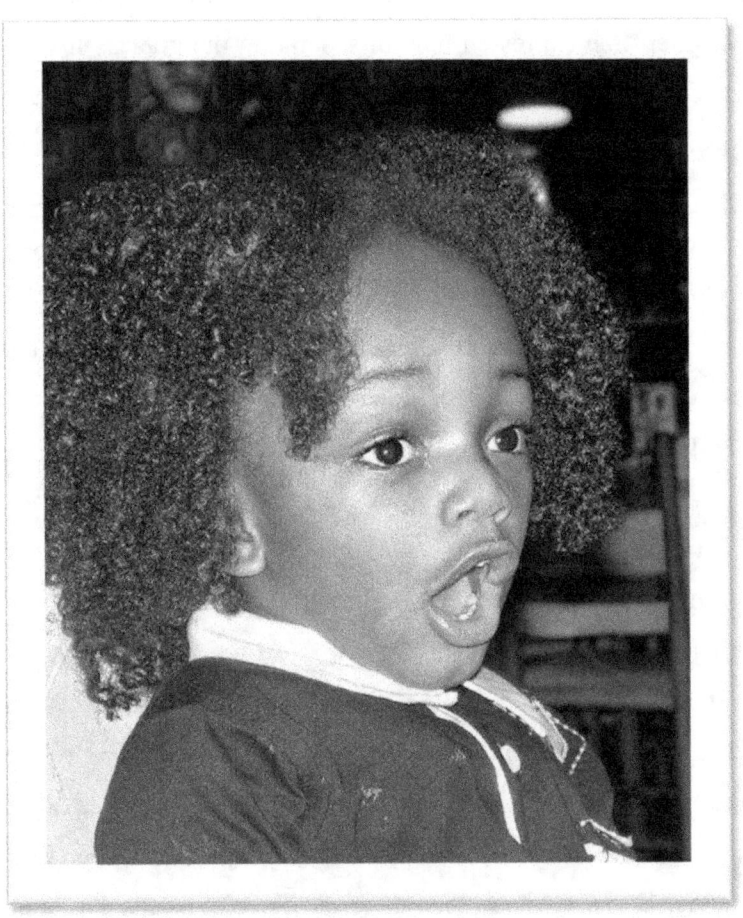

I was having a casual conversation with a Mainstream Mom, and she was telling me about how in her daughter's School District she would go to two different schools for Middle School. She said her daughter would first go to a campus for grades 6th through 7th, and then another campus for 8th – 9th, and then finally to High School. When she told me that, my heart immediately started racing at even the thought of Caleb having to do something like that!

She went on to say how excited she was about their District breaking up the middle school time, and what a great benefit it was for her daughter. She expressed how in separating the grades, this would allow her daughter to ease into middle school and the next phase of life, as she was dealing with puberty and all the hormonal life changes at that stage.

As soon as she mentioned those multiple campus changes, my thoughts at once went to Caleb and how devasting it would be for him to go through so many back-to-back changes with new teachers, classrooms, students, and all the other things associated with it. I couldn't see for one second how the benefits she mentioned that were going to be helpful for her daughter would be in any way beneficial for My Caleb.

I had an epiphany at that moment. I realized how we are both existing in the same universe, but our lives and views are completely different. Yes, I am walking, talking, existing, and participating in this thing we call life, as we all know it; but I am also coexisting in a world that deals with IEPs and ARDs and BIPs and PT, ST, OT, ABA, Transition Plans and Services, and all the many other things that pertain to our Autism and Special Needs World. Managing both can be a huge daily challenge. Mainstream Friends and Family Members expect us to operate in the same manner as them when it comes to our Special Needs Children; yet they have no idea how hard it is to continually meet the needs of our children while trying to remain connected to Mainstream Society.

We are so engrossed in 'our' universe. The sounds that Caleb makes when he's happy; the way he likes to skip a little when he walks;

the way he likes to sway back and forth; the way he likes to grab your face when he likes you or raise his arm and says, 'I want tickles please!', are all common and a part of our daily life. We don't even think twice about them. It is 'normal' for us. It is only when I am pulled out of our everyday 'universe' and am immersed back into the universe of Mainstream Life, that I can see the stark contrast of what Caleb can do in relation to his Mainstream Peers. For me, seeing that vast divide between the two often creates hard realities that carry great pain.

Suddenly, I am pulled out of our world of Autism, and am forced to measure Caleb's growth and behavior by the world's standard. One minute I am celebrating the fact that he asked for his lunch in a 2-word-sentence; the next, I am lamenting the fact that other children his age are conversing on a near adult level and are reading, writing, and comprehending things that Caleb cannot even begin to understand. Facing that reality is very conflicting and can be overwhelming and depressing. It can send you into a tailspin, causing you to neglect recognizing and celebrating your child's accomplishments, because they are such a long way from their Mainstream Peers.

Experiencing those times makes me very sad because I am overwhelmed with the gap I see between Caleb and other Mainstream Children his age. It literally takes my breath away. I start feeling fear and the weight of the uncertainty of what his future is going to be like. In times like this, I allow myself to 'go there' and to feel those feelings. I believe it is always important to do that and to be real with ourselves and acknowledge how we feel.

While I allow myself to go there, I also know that I cannot remain in that state. I know I must eventually pick myself back up mentally and focus on Caleb and the things that he is doing and accomplishing. And, most importantly, I must never, ever compare him to any other child, albeit Special Needs or Mainstream. Doing so would be setting him up to fail because he is his own person, on his own timetable, walking his own life's path.

Living, breathing, and striving to navigate in both our Special Needs Universe, and that of the Mainstream, is one of the most exhausting things anyone could ever do. Our friends and family members inadvertently want us to exist only in one world, their Mainstream World, but we cannot. Even if we wanted to, we cannot.

Case in point, A Mainstream Parent may want to plan a spur-of-the-moment get together for the children at a waterpark, zoo, at someone's house, or another public venue. What they don't understand is, while they may be able to get their children ready, pack some lunches, and be at the location in an hour, we Special Needs Parents must first gauge our child's mood to see if it's a good day/time for them to go. We must consider the venue and if it will be too loud, too bright, or too big for our child's senses to not be overwhelmed. If they wear noise-cancelling headphones, we must make sure we have them.

If they take medication, we must consider how long we will be gone before their next dose is due. We also must make sure we have the proper package to store it in, especially if it needs to remain cold. We must make sure our child has on the proper clothing for the event, and the texture of their clothes will not start to irritate them after a while from being in an environment that is too hot or too cold.

As we consider the size of the venue we are going to, and think about the fact that despite our best efforts, our child may become lost or separated from us. If their speech is limited or they are nonverbal, this causes us a lot of anxiety and grave concern. How will the Lost and Found know how to reach us if our child cannot tell them who they are? If our child is on a special diet or is a picky eater, we must take their food with us and have time to prepare it before we go. In the five minutes it took for a Mainstream Friend or Family Member to suggest this spur-of-the-moment outing, these are just some of the things that go through Special Needs Parents' minds as we consider taking part. Based on all the things aforementioned, it's no wonder many Special Needs Parents would decline the offer.

For those Special Needs Families who would choose to go to the impromptu outing, they would likely not be able to fully relax and enjoy it. They would spend most of their time subconsciously 'holding their breath' trying to predict all the things that might happen with their children and then try to run interference before they do. Especially, if the place they are going to is somewhere they have not been previously with their child.

Once they get back to the car and then home, they would finally be able to exhale because they got through the entire event without their child having a meltdown in public and everyone watching and judging; they are relieved because they didn't find themselves in a situation where they needed something for their child and didn't have it; and they and their child made it back home safely and in one piece.

I shared this very realistic scenario in the hopes that my Mainstream Friends and Family Members can really grasp the concept of what our lives are like in raising our Special Needs Children. These events I described are not something that we have to deal with on occasion but rather our daily reality. I can understand how if you didn't have this knowledge, it would be easy to be critical of us Special Needs Parents when we decline to participate in events. And how it is very difficult to understand the world we live in.

Before I had Caleb, I was always empathetic to those who had children with Special Needs. I must shamefully say, however, I didn't understand what it took to manage their daily lives. And because of that, I likely would have been the Mainstream Mom inviting the parent to the "spur-of-the-moment outing," and then being upset because I didn't understand why they couldn't 'just put the children in the car' and come. Now that I live this life every day, I am much more understanding when my Mainstream Friends and Family Members get upset when Caleb and I, or our entire family, can't always come to their functions. I just take into consideration the fact that they truly do not understand what it takes for us to get there.

As the years have passed, and Caleb's growth and development has progressed, I have become more comfortable in this role of a parent with a Special Needs Child. There is never a moment where you 'figure it all out' and then keep moving from there. There are some lessons you come to learn from experience. I have found that planning and anticipation of need are one of the most critical things to help me manage our day-to-day lives.

CHAPTER FOUR

A GLIMPSE INTO MY WORLD:

"DAILY CHALLENGES"

I f one were to take a glimpse into my world and observe the Daily Challenges I regularly face while raising Caleb, you would see even the most common things can sometimes seem insurmountable and be extremely overwhelming. Routine things like going to the doctor, having medical tests run, finding adequate childcare, therapy changes, family events, outings, and so much more, can completely exhaust both Caleb and I for an entire day.

Attempting to effectively manage Caleb's appointments and events, while minimizing his reactions during the processes, can be monumental tasks. A simple outing to places Caleb has gone to and enjoyed a hundred times before, can suddenly become major disasters. A trip to a medical imaging center for a quick scan can lead to an all-day event. A sudden need for childcare can be the biggest roadblock. There is nothing easy about the Autism Journey that we walk daily, nor for all the obstacles and challenges we must work so hard to overcome to make sure our children get what they need.

Here is a glimpse of some of those Daily Challenges I have experienced with Caleb.

DAILY CHALLENGES: "A Fun Day Out"

ALL ROADS LEAD TO LOVE

By nature, I am a Planner and a Coordinator. I proudly consider myself to be the "Family Concierge!" I absolutely love planning outings and events for my family: from dinners and eating out, to pictures in the bluebonnets during the spring, holiday pictures at various Christmas events in the winter, fall outings with the pumpkins at local Arboretums, and capturing fun times and making new memories by the pool during the summer. I firmly believe it is not always the big things that bring about the best memories, but often the smaller things and great quality family time.

As we neared the end of summer and Caleb returning to school, I I wanted us to do something fun and exciting nearby. We decided to go to the Embassy Suites, one of our local favorites. I planned everything, including us all wearing matching colors, spending time in the pool, lounging in the hot tub, enjoying the Manager's Reception, the impressive breakfast buffet, and all the other amenities.

My husband Curtis and I decided since Caleb loves to jump so much, we would start our Weekend Staycation by taking him to a Trampoline Park. While it had been some time since Caleb had been jumping, he had been to this place before, and absolutely loved it! We all piled into the car and headed over to the Park. I was so excited! I couldn't wait to see the look of joy and excitement on Caleb's face as he was jumping and soaring in the air!

We chose to go to the Park when they first opened before it got too crowded. This time had always worked best for Caleb, so he could jump freely without too many other children running around. When we got inside, Caleb was acting a little shy, like he sometimes does when he goes somewhere new, or hasn't been to a place in a while. He had his arms wrapped around my waist and was holding on to me. I kept soothing him to keep him calm telling him, *"Look, Caleb! You get to go jump!"* I was trying to get him excited. We went into the Park, put on our jumping socks, and I headed over to the jumping mat.

Normally, when we go, Caleb is running to the mat. This time, he pulled back. For a second, it caught me off guard. I never expected that reaction in a million years. I was in no way prepared to respond to it. I gently started trying to coax Caleb to come over to the mat with me. He would walk a few steps towards it, and then start pulling back. I could see the anxiety and fear building in his face and in his body language. I was perplexed. I had no idea what to do. This was the first time I had experienced this reaction from Caleb when doing an activity I knew he loved.

I tried going to the mat and jumping myself, hoping he would want to come join me. He stood a few feet away from me, jumping up and down on the concrete, in unison with me, but he wouldn't come out on the mat. I got down on my knees on the mat and reached my hand out to him, hoping that would ease his fears to come over. He walked a few steps towards me, then turned around. I stood partially on the floor and on the mat, trying to get him to come to me. That didn't work either. Curtis gave him a quarter to bring to me on the mat; he brought it over and stretched his arm out as far as he could, to give it to me, without getting on the mat. I finally went over and got it from him.

We did this off and on for the thirty minutes we were there. His feet never touched the mat. To some people, this might not seem like such a big deal, but to me it was huge. There are so few things that our Special Needs Children can do, that come so easily for Mainstream Children. Jumping was one thing I knew Caleb loved so much! So, I knew if he just put one foot on that mat, he would 'remember' this was something he enjoyed. That is why I tried so hard to get him out there.

No matter how much I knew Caleb would enjoy jumping, I would never force him to do anything he didn't want to do. He is a human being with his own thoughts, feelings, and desires, and I respect that. I had to respect the fact that in that moment, for whatever reason, he could not overcome his fears to get out there and jump. It was at this time we decided to leave.

Afterwards, I went through all kinds of emotions. I felt angry. Not at Caleb, but at the fact that he was having to deal with this Disorder called Autism and it was stealing a moment of joy and fun from my son. I felt confused. In times like these, my natural inclination is to go into a very logical mode. My mind says, *'Caleb loves to jump. We are at the jumping place. There's the mat. Caleb Go Jump'*. I then must remind myself that logic often has no place in the process of Caleb dealing with Autism and the things that are going on in his mind and heart.

I felt so sad. I saw all the other children Caleb's age running and laughing, carefree and having a good time, and I wanted so badly in my heart for it to be the same for him. I felt frustrated. I am a problem solver and used to being able to bring things to a resolution. But in this case, everything I tried failed. I felt helpless. I just wanted to cry.

It was hard for me to finally agree with Curtis for us to go ahead and leave. I didn't want to give up. I wanted to keep trying. I didn't want Caleb to mis that fun moment. Even though I had absolutely no control over what happened, I felt like the worst mother in the world. After we left, we went and enjoyed an awesome breakfast. Caleb ate twice as much food as he normally does. After we saw this, the only thing Curtis and I could conclude was, perhaps Caleb was just hungry, and it was affecting his mood. It took me a few hours to get over what happened and to put it behind me and move forward. When we got back to the hotel, Caleb had no further problems, no mood changes, no fear, or confusion, just fun! We all enjoyed the rest of an amazing weekend.

I learned a lot of lessons that day including, even with our best intentions and the most careful planning, we cannot always predict the outcome. And the best way to deal with unexpected behaviors and challenges is to remain loving, calm, and reassuring, to ensure our children undoubtably know there is nothing they can ever do to lose our love.

About a week later, we took Caleb back to the same Trampoline Park. I wanted to try again. Sure enough, as soon as we walked in and took off our shoes, Caleb went straight to the mat and started jumping. He had a Blast! I have to say, I enjoyed that moment even more because of what had happened before. It filled my heart with JOY to see the big smile on Caleb's face as he jumped and soared high in the air!

I entitled this section, *'A Glimpse into My World'* because these are the kind of situations that can turn our children's lives upside down. It makes me saddest because whatever is occurring in our children's lives in that moment of frustration, might be a simple irritant that can easily be resolved. When their speech and communication is limited, however, they have no way of telling us these things so we can help them. Instead, we Special Needs Parents must go through a myriad of reasons in our minds as to what might be wrong, and we don't always know if we've figured it out correctly or not. Additionally, we never know what behaviors will arise from these unexpected occurrences, which makes it even harder to be prepared.

It took me five years to complete my Doctorate. As grueling and intense as that process was, I can still say, raising a child with Special Needs is one of the hardest things I've ever done. Most of the time it takes everything in you to be able to endure. That endurance often comes from having more patience than you ever imagined possible. It comes from having to pull from your last ounce of strength when your heart is breaking. It comes from hugging your child, kissing their forehead, and telling them everything is going to be okay, when you are wondering in your mind how that is going to be so. It comes from turning your face towards your child and greeting them with a huge smile, when inside you feel worn out and tired. It comes from having to sometimes repeat the same phrases, or watch the same movies repeatedly, without showing any frustration and responding only in kindness and love.

For all the difficult moments, there are times when your child looks you in the eyes, and you see their love without them ever saying a word. When I ask Caleb if he loves Mommy, he grabs my face with both his hands and leans his forehead towards me for a kiss. Or he lays his cheek against my cheek. That is his way of saying *'Yes, Mommy. I Love You.'* His deliberate actions to show me how he feels, means a thousand times more to me than any words he could say.

There are times when Caleb and I are in public, and he becomes apprehensive or afraid. During those times, he will wrap his arms around me and draw nearer to me. He does this because he trusts me. I represent safety to him. There is no greater honor in this life than for me to walk in this role. It is an honor to know that GOD Almighty chose me to care for Caleb, one of HIS most precious jewels who cannot completely care for himself.

There are many times when I must fan the flames of hope to encourage myself that one day things will turn around for Caleb, and he will be able to live a full and productive life. I have learned to take each moment and live them one by one, and deal with them as they are in that moment. I have learned to have a short memory and to not linger on the things that didn't go the way I had hoped. I have learned what I had hoped for in one moment, might occur in the next. I have learned to keep things timely and relevant and to always be ready.

DAILY CHALLENGES*: "Dealing with the Unexpected"*

Anytime you are raising a child with Special Needs, particularly those on the Autism Spectrum, any kind of change, even the most minor ones, can turn your entire world upside down. To mitigate the effects of those changes, you must try to predict what might happen beforehand and then assess how your child may react to or feel about the change. You must also consider ways and things you can do to minimize the change and ease them into it as much as possible.

Even while doing everything, you can to prepare your child for an event, there are always going to be things to occur that you had not considered. Sometimes, our children's reaction to a change is minimal and nothing like we expected. And other times, their reaction is much greater than we ever imagined. In any case, dealing with change is one of the most unpredictable and unnerving situations to be in. During these times, I find myself doing a dancing act of trying to remain calm and keep control of the situation, while trying to find a quick solution to the problem. Caleb watches my reactions, and he feeds off my energy. I often set the tone of how he will react to unexpected occurrences.

Case in point: We had been on the same PPO Insurance Plan for 15 years. During those 15 years, Caleb was seeing the same doctor from his 2-week after-birth appointment, up until age nine. When my husband's company decided to change from a PPO to an HMO, it threw our lives into a tailspin. Unfortunately, when the decision was made to change the insurance, we had no say-so in the matter. Not only did Curtis and I lose our doctors we had known and trusted with our healthcare for 15 years, but Caleb lost the only Pediatrician he had known as well. It was devastating.

The time came when Caleb needed to go see his new doctor for the first time. I did everything I could to prepare him for the appointment. For days I kept talking to him about going to the doctor and that the doctor was going to look at his tummy. I knew the first visit was going to be a challenge, but I was still hoping for the best. As we headed to the appointment, I knew Caleb would have some anxiety about going, simply because it was to a place he had never been before with people he had never met.

While Caleb's speech is limited, his brain is not. He is highly intelligent and very astute. As we drove towards the appointment, I could tell from his face and from him looking around, he immediately knew we were driving in a different direction. Normally, when we leave at that time in the morning, we would be headed to his school. Caleb recognized this time we were not. As we got further down the road, he started to cry a little and showed some anxiety. I kept trying to keep him calm by letting him know we were first going to the doctor, and then he was going to school.

When we got to the doctor's office, Caleb seemed to be okay. He clung to me a little tighter, but I expected this and kept reassuring him that everything was going to be fine. When we got into the waiting room of the doctor's office, Caleb seemed relaxed and okay. He was so relaxed to the point that even I was caught off guard. He enjoyed watching the fish in the fish tank and playing with the toys, everything was going well. I had expected when he saw the new doctor, he might have some anxiety, because he always showed some even when dealing with his previous pediatrician of nine years.

When the nurse opened the door and called us back, Caleb hesitated and pulled away. After some coaxing we were finally able to get him to go into a small room up front in the inner office to check his height and weight. When the time came for us to go back into the examination room to see the doctor, Caleb refused to go. He started pulling away from me. He was scared and crying. As much as I had anticipated beforehand how things might would go, Caleb's reaction still caught me off guard. Since he did so well when we took him back to check his height and weight, I assumed he would do okay when going to the examination room.

The more we tried to get Caleb to go back to the room, the more upset he became. He kept grabbing my hand and pulling me towards the door, letting me know he wanted to leave. I kept telling him it was going to be okay, and that we were going to see the doctor. The nursing staff and I tried giving him toys, offering him juice, and giving him books. We tried everything. Nothing worked. At that moment I felt completely helpless and inadequate as a mother. Everything I had anticipated doing, should any situations arise, had been completely exhausted. I tried not to show my anxiety, to help keep the situation calm, but it was hard. I'm sure I didn't do a very good job. This situation was new to me, and I simply did not know what else to do to fix it.

I called my husband at work and asked him to talk to Caleb to reassure him. That seemed to help some. Caleb would go a few steps further towards our assigned room but would then turn around and go back into the lobby. As you can imagine, my stress level was building fast. This was our first time in the doctor's office with this staff, and I had no idea what their reaction would be to Caleb holding up their schedule. You never know how people are going to react to your Special Needs Child when confronted with these kinds of situations. Some people are empathetic and reassuring, while some are visibly agitated and annoyed.

Thankfully, the office staff was wonderful! The nurse and the office manager both came into the lobby and tried to connect with Caleb to help calm him down. They kept telling me it was okay, and he could take as much time as he needed to feel comfortable. They didn't make me feel rushed to get him back to the room, and even offered to reschedule the appointment for later that afternoon or the next day if we couldn't get him to go back. At this point, I was exasperated. I had tried everything I could think of, and nothing worked. I felt so inefficient as a parent.

After the staff told me that we could allow Caleb some time to just relax in the lobby and try to become more comfortable, I felt better. The doctor even offered to come and see Caleb in the lobby, if necessary. At that time, he and I were the only ones in the lobby. It really touched my heart and meant a lot to me that the doctor was willing to do this.

I called Caleb over and said, *'Let's pray to Jesus.'* He knows who Jesus is; he understands prayer; and he always ends them by saying 'Amen.' I prayed that GOD would help Caleb to go back to see the doctor and HE would send HIS angels to walk back there with him and help him to not be afraid. Suddenly, one thing occurred to me as I was sitting there with him. The hallway we were trying to get Caleb to walk down had a bend that you couldn't see around. When Caleb went back for his height weight check, I remembered there was a second hallway on the other side that went straight back from the lobby door into the examination room.

When we were trying to get Caleb to go down the first hallway, the one that had the bend, as soon as he got near the corner, he would turn and go back. I realized it was because he couldn't see what was around the bend! So, it occurred to me to try walking down the long straight hallway that went right into the examination room to see if Caleb would follow me. Sure enough, he did! I started walking, and he followed me. We turned and our room was right there. With a little coaxing Caleb came into the room. The doctor came in shortly thereafter and examined Caleb. He was good with him, and Caleb liked him. I was so relieved!

When we left the doctor's office, I took Caleb to school. He was back in his routine and very happy to be there. I, on the other hand, was mentally exhausted and had a headache for the rest of the day. I replayed the scenario of what happened over and over in my mind, trying to figure out what I could have done differently, and how I could have been better prepared for the situation.

Of course, I could have always remained calmer. When handling unknown situations like this, I immediately have that feeling of going into panic mode. I am overcome by fear that I won't be able to figure out what to do to resolve them. I realized I was being too hard on myself and that I was as prepared for that moment as I could have been. When we arrived, Caleb seemed like he was going to be okay, and then suddenly things took a turn.

I must admit there are times when I don't understand Caleb's processes. I just know this is the way his mind works, and I must respect that about him as a human being. As crucial as it was for our appointment to be successful and for Caleb to see the doctor, there was no way I was going to grab him and drag him back into the doctor's office. First, he shouldn't be forced to do anything. Also, I knew if I ever did anything like that, he would never want to go back to that doctor's office again. I had to allow him to work on his timetable, not mine.

Later that evening, we went on a pre-scheduled family outing to the local Planetarium for a Christmas show. We had never been there before. I thought it would be something fun to do as a family to launch the start of the Holiday Season. After what had happened earlier at the doctor's office, I expected Caleb might have some difficulty being there. I knew there were going to be times during the Show where the room would be completely dark (when showing the nighttime 'stars'), and it might be loud at times. I was watchful of his reactions and a bit on edge.

When the Show started, Caleb seemed to be oblivious to all those things. It was as if he had been there many times before. He was in awe of the Christmas lights on the dome screen and the music. He just kept looking around in wonderment. I waited to see if any moments of anxiety would come, and there were none. He sat in the theater the entire time between his dad and I, calm and peaceful.

He never showed any anxiety from being in the dark, enclosed, loud theater. These are all things that would typically overload our Autism Children's senses. I have to say, once again, I was completely caught off guard, but in a good way. After watching Caleb for a bit longer and realizing he was going to be okay, I breathe a sigh of relief and Thanked GOD there weren't any issues.

The dichotomies of raising a child with Autism are this: On one hand, I had a situation with Caleb at the doctor's office where it seemed everything would go smoothly, and it didn't. While, on the other hand, I had another situation at the Planetarium, where children with Autism typically have problems from sensory overload, and Caleb did perfectly fine. I learned; at the end of the day, we never know what is going to happen. We must take things as they come and do the very best, we can with what we have.

Some people would look at Caleb's behavior in the doctor's office, and would wonder what was wrong with him? They would judge him and say he was misbehaving and a bad child. They would also judge me as a mother and say I couldn't control my child and needed to discipline him. What they don't understand is the anxiety and fear our Special Needs Children feel are real. Not only is it real, but it is heightened when our children are confronted with situations of the unknown. In their minds, the world works a certain way, and anything outside of that way or routine makes them feel like something is wrong.

I've learned during those times when things seem unfamiliar, as much as Caleb loves and trusts me, my coaxing and reassuring him that everything will be okay, sometimes only goes so far. Oftentimes, I must allow him the time and space to work through the situation he is confronted with in his own mind and come to a resolution and peace within himself. I cannot do it for him. He must work through it until he feels the unexpected situation is okay and won't harm him. Waiting for Caleb to come to this conclusion takes an immense amount of patience and cannot be rushed. I've learned, trying to rush him through this process tends to prolong the situation and makes it worse.

It is Caleb's desire to make sense of the world, and to keep things intact as he believes they should be, that makes me have an even greater love for him. Naturally, I know that our world is anything but predictable and is always changing. I try with all my might, however, to keep Caleb's world as close to what he considers 'normal' as possible. For those times when I know his 'normalcy' is going to be disrupted or changed, I do everything within my power to help soften the blow.

This is a Glimpse into my life and some of its Daily Challenges. As crazy as it sometimes is, I wouldn't trade it for the world. Because to do so would mean that I wouldn't have My Caleb. I would rather have him with all of life's challenges, than to ever spend one single moment without him. Sometimes, in dealing with these challenges I come through as the highly decorated champion, and other times as a weak decimated foe just happy to have survived the moment. Each time, I walk away from a better, stronger, and more compassionate person. In every situation Caleb and I face, my love for him continues to grow, and I remain in awe at the depths of the love I have for him.

DAILY CHALLENGES: "Finding A Safe Place for Caleb"

Imagine having a child with Special Needs. Imagine having a child whose speech is limited, or they are completely nonverbal. Imagine having a child whose cognitive ability and reasoning are hindered because of their Special Needs. Imagine being in a position where you must work and leave that child in the care of strangers. Imagine dropping them off at a day care with workers you hope won't abuse them or mistreat them. Imagine having a 4-year-old child who is not fully potty trained.

What would you do in this situation? How could you possibly have any peace throughout your workday knowing your Special Needs Child is in this situation and cannot tell you what is occurring if anything is wrong? These scenarios are a Glimpse of the Daily Challenges and issues we Special Needs Parents are confronted with on a regular basis.

After his Autism Diagnosis, Caleb started his half year of Pre-K after the Thanksgiving Break. Before going to school, he had never gone to daycare nor stayed with a stranger. He had only been with me, and one in-home babysitter, Mrs. Campbell. She is an older African American Lady who did private sitting. She was an excellent caregiver and someone I trusted completely.

Caleb loved going to her home. She took such great care of him and gave me peace of mind. I don't know what I would have done without her. This lady has poured her whole life into caring for children. She is loved by so many and has raised two to three generations in one family of parents, their children, and grandchildren. Mrs. Campbell was a Godsend! Because of her, Caleb's childcare was never an issue in the beginning.

Once Caleb started kindergarten and was in school all day, I was thankfully able to adjust my work schedule to go an hour earlier so that I could be home to meet his bus. That worked out well during the school year. As the summer break was fast approaching, however, I was confronted with the major issue of finding a place to care for Caleb since he would soon be home all day. Because I worked full time, I suddenly had to find a safe, dependable, and trustworthy place that would care for him in my absence.

A good husband and wife friend of ours, Jennifer, and Robert, watched Caleb during the summers after kindergarten and first grade. Jennifer was trained to work with our Special Needs Children, as she worked as a Special Education Paraprofessional in our district. They both knew Caleb well and were great at working with him. They were excellent with Caleb and instrumental in helping us finally getting him fully potty-trained. They totally alleviated my high level of stress and worrying about Caleb while at work, because I knew he was in the best care. Going into the third summer, they moved away and were no longer available to care for Caleb. It was at this time I was confronted with the most stressful situation imaginable: finding safe and adequate childcare for Caleb!

Caleb and I attended a birthday party for one of his classmates. I met a lady there named Yolanda or "Aunt Yo." Caleb's classmate's parent knew her well because Aunt Yo provided daycare services for her son, who also has Autism. Aunt Yo immediately took to Caleb, and he to her. I watched how she interacted with the children. They all loved her so much. She was a natural with them! After briefly mentioning my childcare dilemma to her, Yolanda gave me her business card for her in-home daycare business before we left the party. She told me while most of the children who attended were Mainstream, she was a former PPCD teacher and was totally comfortable watching Caleb, if needed.

Even after seeing her interacting with Caleb and the other children, I was still a bit skeptical. It had absolutely nothing to do with Yolanda. It's just so hard for us Special Needs Parents to let our children go into any environment without us being present. We always worry about their safety, and we want them to be okay.

As the school year was about to end, I began calling different daycares to see if they would accept Caleb for their summer program. At that time, I had forgotten about Aunt Yo. The main issues I ran into when calling the daycares were, not all of them had staff that were trained to deal with our Special Needs Children, but they said they were sure he would be "okay." And the ratio of children to teachers was extremely high. They also said Caleb needed to be fully potty trained, and he needed to be able to tell them when he had to go to the bathroom. Even if I had been willing to accept the earlier conditions listed (which I was not), there was no way around the potty-training issue – him being fully potty trained and being able to tell them when he needed to go.

At that time, we were working fervently on the potty-training issue, and while Caleb was almost there, he was still needing assistance. We were also working on a *"Go Potty"* phrase for him to use when needing to go, but he hadn't quite mastered it yet. He just needed a little more time to get there. Unfortunately, time was not on our side. I called several daycares, and they all said the same thing. I was in a state of panic and despair and totally at a loss on what to do.

After much prayer and seeking GOD on what I needed to do, I eventually remembered Aunt Yo! Thankfully, I found her business card and reached out to her. I asked if she had any openings, and she said 'Yes!' We arranged for me to bring Caleb to her home to see how he would react. As we walked into Yolonda's house, I at once felt a calmness and peace. Caleb took his shoes off and walked around looking at everything. She encouraged us to both do this. When it was time to leave, Caleb pulled away. He didn't want to go. His reactions told me all I needed to know.

I rely a lot on his reactions and intuition when placed in unknown situations and in dealing with strangers. I could tell he felt safe and comfortable there. My heart was happy! When I was finally able to get him to the door to leave, Caleb gave Aunt Yo the biggest hug. I knew I had found the right place for him!

During his summertime spent with Aunt Yo, Caleb flourished! She treated him just like all the other children. She made sure he was included and involved in all the activities; she showed him so much loved; she genuinely cared for him. Every day when I dropped Caleb off in the mornings and went to pick him up after work, all I could do was Thank GOD for allowing me to find Aunt Yo. My heart was overcome with gratitude. She was such a blessing to us!

Caleb and I both enjoyed him going to Aunt Yo's so much, once school started back, I arranged for his afternoon bus drop-off to be at her house. It allowed him to spend at least two hours with her and the other children in the afternoon before I picked him up after work. It was such a wonderful arrangement. Caleb continued to go to Aunt Yo's house after school and then spent another summer in her care until I started Consulting full time. At that point, he was able to be home with me in the afternoons and during the summer. To this day Caleb has a special love for Aunt Yo, and she for him. They are forever bonded, and I am forever grateful. Finding Aunt Yo was the answer to many fervent prayers, and it alleviated a multitude of anguish and distress.

While I was fortunate enough to find a Safe Place for My Caleb to go, many of our Special Needs Parents are not. Thankfully, after a lot of really hard work, Caleb did become fully potty-trained that summer. Many of our Special Needs Children are not potty-trained, due to a variety of reasons which are beyond their control.

The level of stress we Special Needs Parents must deal with in these situations, along with trying to find adequate childcare, is magnified 100-fold. But like with mine and Caleb's situation, I believe GOD always provides the Aunt Yo's and the answers we need at the exact right time.

DAILY CHALLENGES: "Medical Testing"

Many of our Special Needs Children have chronic health issues that are related to their Autism or other Special Needs Diagnosis. Going to medical appointments, having tests run, and seeing specialists are common occurrences in our world. At one point, Caleb's ongoing digestive/gut issues carried over into his bladder and caused major problems.

Caleb was required to get an ultrasound to not only look at his bladder, but all his major organs, to figure out exactly what was happening. We Special Needs Parents always experience a high level of stress with any medical testing and specialist visits. Mainly because, many of those administering the tests are accustomed to doing things one way to get the outcomes they are seeking. They often expect our Special Needs Children to follow their instructions, take directions, and react like

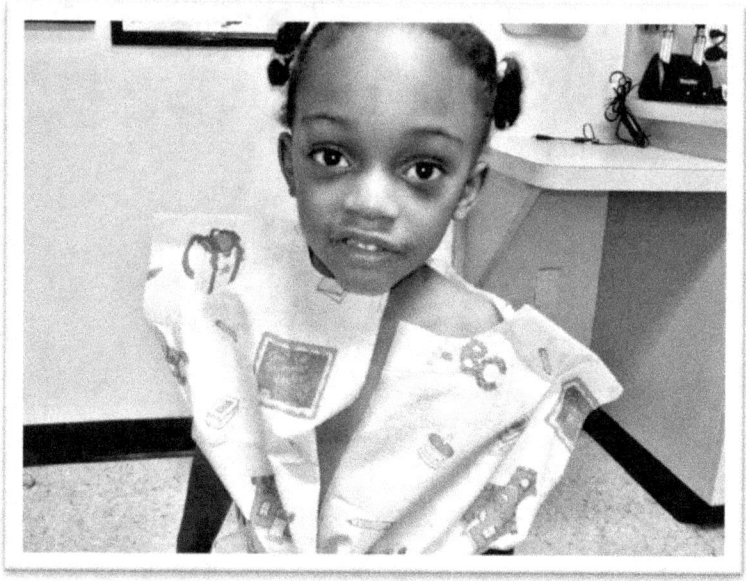

their Mainstream Peers. They often don't want to listen to advice from the parents on the varied ways they can administer the tests to get the results they need.

Caleb started having bladder problems due of his chronic digestive / gut issues. Gut issues are common for children with Autism. I wasn't told until two months after the fact that he had stopped using the bathroom at school. This change resulted in him developing a distended bladder. A failure to notify me of this change made his dad and I unaware of what was happening with him, and it led to Caleb enduring months of pain and spasms. I was furious! The thought of Caleb getting used to holding his urine all day until he got home, was crushing!

It wasn't until Caleb ended up in a Children's Hospital ER with excruciating pain that we discovered this bladder issue. The doctor who treated Caleb said the pain he was experiencing would make a grown man fall to his knees. It was gut-wrenching for me to hear this news, and to know because of Caleb's limited speech, he was not able to tell us what was going on with him. It was heartbreaking seeing him in the hospital dealing with so much pain, knowing it could have been prevented.

After the ER visit, the doctor recommended Caleb to see a Child Urologist. Our insurance first scheduled Caleb to go see an Adult Urologist because a child urologist was not in our network. He at once wanted to do risky surgery on Caleb's bladder by going through the urethra. He admitted this surgery was typically done on adults only, was not fully necessary, and could affect Caleb's ability to one day have children. I told him 'Absolutely not!' I have been confronted with situations like this in the past where some doctors seemingly want to do experimental or risky surgery on our children simply because they have Special Needs. I'm not going to allow anyone to 'practice' or do exploratory surgery on my child. I am always looking out for Caleb's best interest and will not allow anyone to put him in harm's way!

After fighting with the insurance company for over a month, I finally got them to approve for Caleb to see a Child Urologist that was out of network, because ours had none. Thankfully, we found an amazing Child Urologist that Caleb loved. He was very comfortable with her and her staff, and they were caring and understanding of his limitations. On our routine visits, the doctor first performed Caleb's ultrasounds in her office to accommodate him. I told her from the beginning, Caleb would not under any circumstances lie down on the examination table; so, her staff did the ultrasound while he was sitting in the chair.

After the tests did not reveal all the information she needed, the doctor ordered an x-ray. When we went to Radiology, they asked Caleb undress and lie on the table. I explained to them he had Autism and would not under any circumstances lie on the table. The technician went on to explain how they would get the best picture if he was lying down. I told her I clearly understood that, but Caleb was not going to lie on the table. I pointed out to her the doctor had put this in the orders she sent over. The technician said she would call to verify that was the case.

While she was calling, I thought about the fact that people have no idea how hard it is to do even the simplest things for our Special Needs Children. I can clearly understand the fact that someone would say, *'All he has to do is lie down on the table for a few seconds, and then it will all be over.'* To them, it is the simplest thing to do. But to our Special Needs Children, it creates an even greater level of fear and anxiety for them to be in an unknown situation, around a group of strangers, doing something that is unfamiliar to them. Even with me there, Caleb still had a lot of anxiety.

The technician was never rude in this situation. I could just tell she was wondering why Caleb couldn't do something so simple for just a few minutes. She kept making suggestions on ways we could try to get him to lie down, and I kept politely telling her no matter what, Caleb was not going to do it. She had no idea how many times I had been in that same situation before, and how many things we had tried in the past to get him to lie on the table, to no avail.

We Special Needs Parents know our children and their limitations, and no number of 'easy' suggestions of things to do are going to change what our children are willing or unwilling to do. Trying to force them to do something only makes the situation a thousand times worse.

After she called to verify the orders with the doctor, I had to stand in front of the x-ray machine first to show Caleb it was okay; and then we finally got him to stand there as well. I then had to stretch my arms out to show him what he needed to do. He then mimicked me spread his arms out too. Afterwards, I had to move over far enough away from Caleb and the x-ray machine, but still be right there with him so he could see me. My visibility provided him with the security and comfort he needed during the x-ray. After everything was done, they finally got the x-ray. We gave Caleb lots of praise and high fives, and I got him dressed.

I left there feeling exhausted both physically and mentally. I know most Mainstream Parents would say, *'What's the big deal? It was just an x-ray, and they got it done.'* First, while we were still in the lobby, I could tell Caleb was having some anxiety. I was worried about the fact that I couldn't get him to sit down while we were in the waiting room waiting to be called back. I wondered if his anxiety would translate into him not wanting to go back with me when his name was called. Thankfully, he came back with no problem.

After we went back to have the x-ray done, the situation arose about him lying on the table. I try hard not to show my anxiety in situations like this, because I know Caleb reads me closely and he watches my reactions. A lot of times, he will react to situations based on how I respond to them. So, I had the stress and pressure of dealing with all these things going through my mind, while trying to rectify the things happening around us. The last thing I wanted was for Caleb to not get the help he needed because he was not able to do what they were asking, and for us to have to come back. We had driven about 30 minutes to get him to this Children's Hospital. Therefore, I was trying to control all these things happening in my mind at one time, all while consoling Caleb and reassuring him that everything was going to be okay.

I imagine, subconsciously, I was holding my breath the whole time these things were occurring. Not only was I trying to keep Caleb calm, but under control as well. Thankfully, he was in a calmer mood and did not jump all over the place while in the waiting room and when we went back. When we walked out of the hospital, I was finally able to mentally exhale. While we accomplished our reason for going to the Child Urologist, it took everything out of me, both physically and mentally.

A short time after our visit, Caleb's Urologist wanted to have another ultrasound done to do some more extensive testing. Each time we had to go to an imaging center, I explained to the technicians he would not lie down on the table to have it done. They each told me repeatedly how that was the only way they would get the most exact results. I told them I was aware of that, but it wasn't going to change the fact that Caleb wouldn't lie on the table. They went ahead and did the imaging with him sitting in the chair and moving all over the place. As I expected, the results came back inconclusive. In the meantime, the nurse at Caleb's pediatrician's office and I were relentlessly petitioning the insurance company trying to get them to approve for him to be sedated for the ultrasound. We knew this would be the only way we could get the correct results we needed.

After three additional ultrasounds, with Caleb moving and sitting in a chair and the results all coming back as inconclusive, the insurance company finally agreed to the sedation several months later. I am not one who is eager to have my child put under sedation and would normally avoid it at all costs. In this case, however, Caleb had been suffering in pain for months, and while the doctor thought she was on course with the right treatment for him, she needed an exact ultrasound to be sure there were no other issues occurring in any of his other major organs. So, it was for that reason I fought so vehemently for Caleb to receive approval for it.

Once the sedation ultrasound was done, we were able to get an exact picture of Caleb's bladder and other major organs, and we were finally able to get him the precise treatment he needed. It was so upsetting to me that it took months before we could make sure Caleb's medical issues were adequately addressed. This delay happened because many in the medical and insurance society refuse to recognize Caleb's Special Needs and only want to treat him based on their protocols. They did not want to take his Autism and limitations into consideration. No parent should ever have to spend as much time as I did to make sure their child gets the medical treatment they need and are entitled to receive.

I shared this Glimpse of our Daily Medical Challenges with you because so often medical professionals don't want to listen to Special Needs Parents. They think most of what we say about our children is made up or all in our heads. They can be condescending and belittling, and try to discount, minimize, or even blatantly ignore the things we say. The advocacy and battles we Special Needs Parents must endure to make sure our children get the care, services, and things they need, spans across all our daily situations, events, and circumstances including, at the doctor's office, schools, eating out in restaurants, going to the grocery store, in social situations, and so much more.

I truly believe most medical professionals' reactions and the way they treat us Special Needs Parents are based primarily on the fact that our children either can't speak or their speech is limited. For some reason, these professionals act as if we parents can't possibly know what is going on with our children because they can't tell us. What they don't understand is, we have a Ph.D., an M.D., and a Psy. D. when it comes to understanding our children's behaviors, actions and gestures, and in interpreting the things they cannot say.

It's a great responsibility having someone totally dependent upon you for what could be the period of a lifetime. Some might question if the parent would be willing to bear such a heavy load? For most of us Special Needs Parents, it is never a question of whether we are willing to do all the things that are needed for our child. The love that I have in my heart for Caleb does not even allow the question to enter my mind. Now, there may be times where I ask myself 'if' I have the strength to do it? Or 'how' will I do it?' But, never, 'will' I, do it? Every time I do what is needed for Caleb, I find that in my Acts of Service towards him, my capacity to love him has increased to yet another level, I never knew existed.

DAILY CHALLENGES: "Facing Painful Decisions"

When Caleb was Diagnosed with Autism, I heard from everyone about the importance of getting him into therapy as quickly as possible. The thought was, by getting him private speech, occupational, and ABA therapy, some of the challenges and behaviors he was confronted with might be mitigated, or even eliminated, in time. While the suggestions were not presented as a way to 'cure' Autism, there was an underlying theme that they could possibly improve Caleb's learning and behavior; thereby giving him a better chance at an independent life.

My main concern with Caleb's Autism Diagnosis was the Speech Impairment Diagnosis that went along with it. While I knew Autism was a huge challenge, I felt like if we could address his speech issue and find an effective way for him to communicate, it could make

Living with Autism easier. So, I got Caleb into private 1-1 Speech, Occupational and Music Therapy sessions, and then later signed him up for ABA (Applied Behavior Analysis) services as well.

For years, I drove Caleb to these therapies twice a week. Each session was usually 30 minutes to an hour long, in multiple surrounding cities. Even though this was a tiring and sometimes grueling process, and most Special Needs Parents do it, I never lost hope that Caleb would one day have that developmental breakthrough and things would get better for him. Oftentimes, when my energy was depleted, maintaining hope for this change was the only thing that kept pushing me to get him from place to place.

After years of being committed to getting Caleb to these therapies, at some point I found myself confronted with the fact that his grant that had paid for three years of his sessions was about to be depleted of funds. A typical 30-minute speech session for Caleb costs about $300 with most

Providers. It's bad enough that we Special Needs Parents must deal with the day-to-day challenges of raising our children, but we also have the added stress and pressure of trying to find ways to afford the services and help that they desperately need. I believe some Providers take advantage of the fact that we parents would do anything to help our children have a better quality of life; so, they charge us astronomical fees for their services.

When faced with the reality of Caleb possibly losing his speech services, I felt all kinds of emotions. A part of me was afraid because I had to face the fact that he was getting older, and we still had not identified a clear means of communication for him. While he had some speech and language, it was still very limited and certainly not enough for him to be able to advocate for himself. I worried about how Caleb was going to be able to speak up for himself. How was he going to function in this world adequately as an adult if he was not able to carry on a conversation? How was he going to express his wants and needs if I was not there to help him?

The weight of all these things hit me at once and completely overwhelmed me. I felt so sad and powerless. All I could do was cry. I thought about all the years of speech therapy Caleb had received, and yet, here we were, seemingly still in the same place. I thought about all the years of driving miles and miles, city-to-city, taking Caleb wherever he needed to go to get the help he needed, and seemingly to no avail. It looked like we had nothing to show for all our efforts. I felt like a complete failure. I cried for Caleb's present and his future, as it seemed so uncertain as to what they would hold.

A part of me felt like I was indirectly giving up on Caleb's ability to ever be able to fully speak. While I knew in the depths of my soul that was not the case, nor would it ever be, I still felt it, nonetheless. I just wasn't ready to give in to what some in our Autism world call a reality: If your child hadn't spoken by a certain age, they likely will not. The thought of ever accepting that philosophy pierced me to the core.

As a Special Needs Parent, every time I've had to abandon an expectation for Caleb, or to even put it on hold, it feels like death. I go through a grieving process for all the things I always hoped for him that seem like they may never happen. My heart hurts incessantly because I know in order for Caleb to do even a modified version of a task, he will have to work 1000 times harder to make it happen in relation to his Mainstream Peers, if it happens at all.

As heartbreaking as it was for me to think about the loss of speech therapy for Caleb, I realized I had to face an important fact: Caleb was getting older, and I needed to start shifting my mindset and expectations and accept the fact that there were now more important things for him to focus on learning. I had to face the fact that he needed to start learning the most basic functional and daily living skills, to better prepare him for living independently as an adult. So, instead of my focusing fully on him being able to read and write and carry on a conversation, I had to start thinking about making sure he knew how to shower, brush his teeth, use a microwave, wash his clothes, clean his room, dress himself, take his medication, and all the other important daily living skills.

This change in thought and strategy felt like another form of death and the abandonment of the possibility that Caleb would one day be more aligned with his Mainstream Peers in their education and learning. I talked to GOD throughout this process. I told HIM I felt like Caleb, and I were being put in a situation where we could not win; and that I was being set up to fail because all my efforts to help Caleb seemed futile. I told GOD I felt like I was asking for help for Caleb and getting no response. I felt completely lost. I wanted to sit down in a corner and never move.

I appreciated the fact that GOD allowed me to come before HIM in my weakness and frailties and open my heart to HIM. That HE allowed me to share my hopes for Caleb and my fears that his dreams may never be fulfilled. HE never left me in that broken state. HE allowed me to get it all out, while showering me with HIS Tender Mercies and HIS Lovingkindness. GOD renewed my strength and caused my faith to rise again. I knew that at some point whether I wanted to or not, I had to get up, dust myself off, and figure out what the next steps were for Caleb, because he was counting on me.

At the point when Caleb's grant monies finally ran out, I stopped his speech services. Thankfully, by the time it happened, I had worked through all the emotions and was better prepared for the change. I got through it by telling myself I wasn't abandoning the idea of Caleb one day speaking and communicating, and I would always maintain hope that an effective means for him to do so would be revealed. It gave me greater consolation to know that in redirecting my focus towards Caleb learning more daily living and functional skills, it would give him a better chance at living an independent life.

Having to face these hard truths about getting our Special Needs Children the help and services they need is just a Glimpse into our Daily Lives, the hard decisions we must make, and the many challenges we Special Needs Parents face. We must confront these issues head-on, whether we want to or not. There are no escape hatches for us, no place to run, and no place to hide.

CHAPTER FIVE
"OUR LIVES ARE HARD BUT NOT BLEAK"

As hard as our lives are in raising our Special Needs Children, most of us parents wouldn't trade this life for all the riches in the world. For me, being even one single second without My Caleb would feel like death. There's nothing in this world that could compare to him being here with me. I would give my life without hesitation so he could have his; and if it ever came down to my life over his, it would be his life every time, because there is no way I would want to live in this world without him. Caleb's life matters that much to me.

Therefore, I will carry this load until my knees buckle under the weight, and all I can do is crawl to keep going. I will never, ever, give up on Caleb, nor regret having him. We Special Needs Parents have the same high hopes and expectations for our children just like any Mainstream Parent. We just must be realistic in our approach in recognizing they may meet some of their developmental goals in a few years or may be working on them throughout the course of their lifetime.

I ask you to take a moment to consider the courage Caleb and our Special Needs Children must exercise each day, to go out into a world that is completely foreign to them, and to try to function in that world that is often loud and chaotic and goes against all their senses. They don't choose to remain home in fear and refuse to go out into that vast world; they instead choose to go out day after day, trying again, and again to master the skills that come so easily to their Mainstream Peers.

When Caleb tries something new for the first time, he wants me there. He wants to hold my hand and have me walk him through it. With his hand in mine, he feels safe and is willing to try. After he has spent some time trying new things and becomes more familiar with them, he is then ready to try them on his own. Caleb will then keep trying until the new skills become natural for him. He does not let fear of the unknown stop him. Watching his unending courage and willingness to try makes me feel so proud and brings tears to my eyes.

This innate ability to keep trying and to overcome fear is not only indicative of My Caleb, but of all our Special Needs Children. They want nothing more than to succeed at whatever they are doing, and they will keep trying until they get it right. The look of joy and satisfaction on their faces as they finally complete the task or new skill is indescribable. It is the most priceless moment.

Our children wake up every day and face the challenge of functioning in a body that doesn't always want to cooperate, in a world that was not designed for them. They just want to be loved and included like everyone else. They are unique and special beings. They want to feel like they are a valued part of society. It is the love and the courage that they give to us Special Needs Parents, and to those around them, that makes our difficult days worthwhile. They are the best of us all.

While this Autism Journey is long and treacherous and often daunting, we Special Needs Parents must always remember that no matter what direction this Journey takes us - whether filled with long winding roads, dark unpredictable paths, through lonely unbearable dry deserts, or an occasional oasis by the river's stream - the good will always find us; and All Roads, no matter from the East, the South, the North, or the West, Leads to Love...

CHAPTER SIX
"WORDS OF ADVICE TO THE MAINSTREAM"

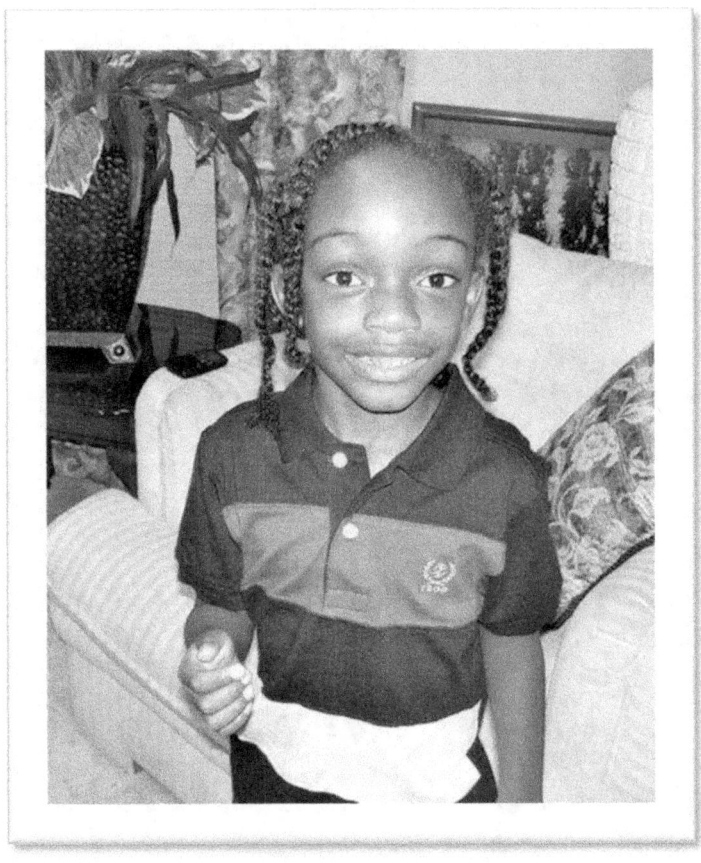

I f you are a Mainstream Person or Parent with any kind of heart of compassion, you must be wondering at this point what you could possibly do to help us Special Needs Parents carry this tremendous load. While some reading this, may not be raising a Child with Special Needs, you probably know someone who is.

I believe knowledge is power. It is my hope that the more you know and understand about our Autism and Special Needs Journey, the more you will feel compelled to offer help and care, or at the very least, compassion. Here is some advice I would like to share with you to help you better understand our Journey and how you can provide support in the most meaningful ways.

ADVICE TO MAINSTREAM: "We Are Doing Our Best"

Please understand when it comes to raising our Special Needs Children, we are doing our very best. There are no shortcuts and there are no breaks. Some days, we may feel triumphant in raising our children and meeting their needs, and others, we may feel inadequate, like we have failed. There is never a moment when it is lost to us how much our children need us and are always counting on us. It is embedded in everything we do and in every decision we make. We don't want your pity. We need your support. We ask you to recognize the heavy load we carry daily and to support us in our efforts, even when you don't always understand our methods.

We know you will not always understand our decisions, and that is okay. We just ask that you please not respond with criticism and unsolicited advice. If there is something you feel you absolutely must say, please consider your timing and do it with tact and grace. You must realize, by the time you unload on us with your harsh tone, judgement, and unwelcome recommendations, we are probably already exhausted, and are likely feeling overwhelmed and distressed. Your words, if not carefully considered, could be the final straw that ultimately breaks our spirit.

ADVICE TO MAINSTREAM: "Please Don't Judge Us"

If you see a Special Needs Parent who has a child of age who should be able to do something simple and can't, please don't judge them. I can assure you, nothing you can conjure up in your mind to say against them, to make them feel belittled or ashamed, could ever come close to all the negative things they are probably already saying to themselves. Instead, please give us the benefit of the doubt and know we are always doing everything we can to bridge the gap between what our child should be able to do, in relation to their Mainstream Peers, versus what they cannot. Oftentimes, these gaps are a sad, glaring reminder, staring us in the face of our children's shortcomings.

Many Mainstream Persons and Parents look at us and judge our situations from the outside looking in, wondering why we keep such tight reins on our children; especially those who are older. Like you, we Special Needs Parents would like nothing better than for our children to be able to sit back, relax, and enjoy their new level of independence and freedom. Unfortunately, while our children's bodies may be growing at the same rate as their Mainstream Peers, their minds often are not. In many cases, our Special Needs Children's chronological age does not always align with their cognitive age, and their physical growth does not always equal maturity.

Therefore, you may see a 5'8" 14-year-old girl with the mental capacity of a 6-year-old child. Because of this dichotomy, many times we must treat our children as if they were younger, even though they are of an advanced age. Regardless of our children's age, we still must be there for them to make sure they are safe and cared for and their needs are met. And in most cases, for those whose speech is limited or nonexistent, we must also be their voice.

It is utterly exhausting feeling like we Special Needs Parents must always be always in all places, to constantly be in a state of anticipation of what might happen to our child, and to feel like we must always have a plan of action to manage it. And, if that is not hard enough, we must do all these things while dealing with harsh criticism and glaring stares, along with feelings of isolation and shame. from others.

ADVICE TO MAINSTREAM: "Don't Kick Us While We're Down"

We Special Needs Parents are far from perfect. I can tell you, however, on our worst days, we are still doing all we can to make sure our children are safe, protected, growing, progressing, and getting everything that they need. For most of us, our goal is to always make sure we are preparing them to live successfully in this big world. Most of the time, we are in a constant state of trying to encourage ourselves to keep going. We also must keep reminding ourselves that the things we do for our children matter and are making a difference, even when it seems they are not. Despite all our hard work and efforts, we often wonder if it is enough or if we are failing them. So, to have a Mainstream Parent, Person, or God-forbid Loved One, come along and criticize all we are doing, and question our decisions for something in which they have no knowledge, can be devastating.

When we encounter moments like these, we Special Needs Parents can feel mentally like we are lying on the ground at our lowest point, wondering how we can go on. Then someone comes along, and instead of kneeling to ask us if we are okay or how they can help us, or extending their hand to help us get up, they 'kick' us while we're down. They kick us with their criticism, judgment, and harsh words.

They lecture us on being a bad or inadequate parent; they tell us what a failure we are; they tell us how much better they would do things if it were 'their' child; they give us unwelcome advice; and, when they leave us, they talk about us to others. While we Special Needs Parents are tough as nails when it comes to raising our children, we still have a heart that can be scarred or broken, just like everyone else.

ADVICE TO MAINSTREAM: "Celebrate Successes with Us"

When dealing with our Special Needs Children, we parents are always working with vast situations that have limited options and outcomes. We are doing all we can to make something beautiful, functional, and meaningful out of all the many challenges our children face daily. So, when we share with you something that our child has done, please celebrate with us. If I tell you Caleb suddenly told me without prompting that he wanted to eat pizza for lunch, please celebrate with me. It may seem insignificant or unimportant to you, but there is probably a long history of him being asked what he wanted to eat, and him not being able to respond. So, the fact that he did so without prompting is a huge success!

Or, if a Special Needs Parent tells you their 8-year-old child used a fork for the first time, please don't minimize or ridicule their accomplishments because you feel the child should have already been using a fork at their age. It is highly likely this child has been practicing this skill thousands of times for many years while in school, at home, and in occupational therapy; and they finally learned it.

If I tell you Caleb allowed me to clip his fingernails for the first time, please celebrate! What you don't know is, for many years, I had to chase him around the house with the clippers. I had to have a two-man system to hold him down while I clipped his nails, and he had a crying fit; or I had to wait for him to fall asleep and then slowly clip one nail at a time like a Stealth Ninja, praying he wouldn't wake up. All the while, I was dealing with the stress and pressure of his teachers and therapists asking me to please cut his nails because he was scratching them. It wasn't that I didn't want to cut his nails, it was just almost impossible to get it done. Therefore, the day I told Caleb to come and sit next to me so I could clip his nails, and he did, it was a BIG DEAL!

Even if you don't understand everything we want to celebrate, or the significance of what is occurring, please just know if we are sharing it with you, that means it is a big deal, and we just want you to be happy with us.

ADVICE TO MAINSTREAM: "We Deserve Respect"

For some reason, it seems like some Mainstream Adults think it's okay to mistreat Parents of Special Needs Children. They act like since our children have challenges, it gives them permission to treat us parents as less. They look down on us; they often openly mock us and ridicule us, and they act as if we are mentally inferior. Some act as if our raising a Special Needs Child gives them permission to say whatever they want and be abrasive in the way they treat or respond to us. These same people, however, would never feel it was okay to treat another Mainstream Parent that way. I can't tell you how many times I have had people use Caleb's Autism Diagnosis and Speech Impairment as a weapon to try and hurt me. Caleb has never done anything against them nor harmed them; and yet they think it's okay to use his condition to hurl insults at me.

I had a lady whom I've known for a long time verbally rebuke me when I told her I had to help Caleb brush his teeth. She was appalled at the fact that at his age, he was not able to do it on his own. I tried to explain to her that most of our Special Needs Children do not learn at the same rate and in the same way as their Mainstream Peers, and it could take years for most of our children to learn even the simplest tasks if they learned them at all. Her response to me was, *"I raised four children and taught them how to do everything, and you can't even teach your one."*

She wasn't interested in the facts I was sharing with her regarding Caleb's learning processes. She dismissed the fact that our children's learning is not a skill or will issue but is rather a brain issue. She instead chose to believe the worst about me and my son. She willingly ignored the fact that even though our children belong to us, we Special Needs Parents are not always trained to teach them in the way that they learn. Therefore, we must rely heavily on therapists who are specialized and trained to teach them. She instead took the things that I shared with her and used it as an opportunity to try and hurt me and tell me I was a bad mother.

When another person, who was supposed to be close to me, got upset with me, she made the statement, *"Your Son can't even talk!"* Again, Caleb has never done anything to her, and her comment had absolutely nothing to do with the issues we were discussing. She said it simply out of spite to try and hurt me.

I could never imagine being so upset with a Mainstream Parent that I would ever feel it was acceptable to outright tell them their child was 'ugly' or 'fat' or something worse. That would be totally unacceptable and inappropriate under any circumstances. And anyone who heard I did such a thing would be completely appalled; and yet we Special Needs Parents have people who feel it's totally acceptable to belittle our children; talk openly bad about them; to use their disabilities as weapons against us; and to treat them as if they are less.

If there is something you feel you need to say to a Special Needs Parent that you would never say to a Mainstream Parent, let that be your indicator that you probably should not say it. Not only is it rude and hurtful to the parent on the receiving end of your vicious words, but our children, who are very intuitive, can pick up on your negative energy towards them as well.

ADVICE TO MAINSTREAM: "Our Children Are Our Gifts"

In a moment of extreme tiredness and weakness and needing to vent, I shared with a Mainstream Mom, who was supposed to be close to me, some of the stresses and challenges I deal with daily in raising Caleb. I talked to her about how hard our lives can be in raising our Special Needs Children, and about how I wondered if I was going to make it. Because she knew of my medical history and difficulties conceiving, she said, *'Maybe I should have listened to the doctor when he told me not to have children and to adopt instead.'* And, *'Had I listened to the doctor, I wouldn't be dealing with all the difficulties of raising a Special Needs Child today.'* She was clearly implying having to raise a child with Autism was my 'punishment' for choosing to go against the doctor's wishes. I couldn't believe what I was hearing!

I immediately let her know, my sharing in a moment of weakness about the things we Special Needs Parents deal with daily was in no way my saying I was sorry I had My Caleb! I told her I would never be sorry nor regret having my son. I told her my Love for Caleb far exceeds any disability or challenges he deals with. I told her I would never trade even one of my hardest days in raising Caleb for one moment without him! And there's nothing in this world that would ever make me sorry or regret having my son!

I'm sure most Special Needs Parents feel this way! The depth of the love we have for our children has no end. Regardless of the events that precipitated our children's arrival with their Special Needs, once they got here, we loved them, and they will never lose our love! We don't see our children as burdens but as blessings. We can say this because we choose to look beyond the dark days and to always find the light. We understand that while it may not always be clear, there is a plan and a purpose for our children's lives. They were sent here for a reason by GOD, and it is Good!

ADVICE TO MAINSTREAM: "Don't Compare Our Child with Another"

Please never, ever, compare one Special Needs Child to another – even those who have the same Diagnosis or disability! It is hurtful and unproductive and does nothing but make us Special Needs Parents feel inadequate and judged.

A person who worked as a substitute teacher in a Special Education inclusion class, often called me after working with her students to ask why Caleb couldn't do certain things. She assumed if her students could do certain things, Caleb should be able to do them as well. I explained to her we were working on many things in his therapies and at school, but there are still many things he's just not able to comprehend at this time.

Because of her limited observations and interactions with Autistic children, she compared the things that Caleb could do with the things her students could do. She told me I wasn't doing my job as a parent in teaching Caleb what he needed to know, and he should be able to do the same things her inclusion students could do. She said Caleb was not able to do these things because I was not teaching him, and I was babying him.

I tried repeatedly to tell her first, all our children are different; and second, she couldn't compare Caleb with her students because they were in an inclusion class. The fact that they were in that type of class meant they were functioning at a different level than Caleb. I explained to her Caleb was currently in a self-contained class, which meant his learning abilities were completely different. I also pointed out the students she was referring to were in high school while Caleb was still in elementary school. She didn't want to hear any of those things, but rather enjoyed telling me what an inadequate mother I was, and how I was failing my child. She took her very limited interactions and views of children dealing with Autism and used them to compare my son with others and to condemn me as a parent.

Just like we Special Needs Parents accept the fact that all Mainstream Children are not the same, we ask you to remember that every Special Needs Child is not the same as well. They each have their own abilities, strengths, and limitations, and should be treated with dignity, respect, and common decency. Unless your intentions are to be deliberately cruel and unkind, please never tell a Special Needs Parent they are failing because their child is not doing something you've read about, saw on a TV show, observed with another child, or encountered in your brief interactions with other Special Needs Children. It is hurtful and unfair.

ADVICE TO MAINSTREAM: "Our Lives Are Different"

I challenge you to stop for a moment and imagine that you had to go against the societal norm in almost everything you did for you and your child. Imagine the looks, the whispers, the stares, and the judgment, not only from strangers, but from those closest to you. Imagine the courage it takes to get up every day and face hostility, not only towards you, but towards your child. Imagine having to repeatedly use all your strength and best efforts to meet the needs of your child, only to be told that you are not doing enough. This is how we Special Needs Parents are made to feel every day by the many people who cross our paths.

The best thing you can do for us Special Needs Parents is to try to understand the peculiar, crazy, unpredictable challenges we face daily, constitutes the makeup of our lives. It is what we know. It is our norm. Your family may have a tradition of everyone gathering around the table on Saturday mornings, eating cereal and talking about your upcoming day. While our family's tradition may consist of our child lining up all their cars across the breakfast table, while eating chicken nuggets and bar-b-que sauce. And instead of talking and planning out our day, we are enjoying watching our child flapping their hands, and rocking back-and-forth, making happy noises. One scenario is no more wrong than the other. It is simply each of our realities.

We Special Needs Families readily accept your Mainstream lives because it is the societal norm and what the Mainstream considers 'right' and 'proper.' We Special Needs Families ask you to open your minds and hearts to realize everyone's life is not lived in black and white; some of us must live life in shades of gray. We are not looking for your pity, just your acceptance. Acceptance in realizing that not everything is the same for everyone, and that is okay. We are no more wrong in our approach in the way we live our lives, than you are in yours.

ADVICE TO MAINSTREAM: "We Don't Have All the Answers to Your Questions"

Please do not flood us with an onslaught of questions on why our children have Special Needs? What caused it? And what we are doing about it to 'fix' it? First, it is rude. It would be no different than me asking a Mainstream Parent why their child was overweight? What caused them to be that way? And what were they doing to help them to lose weight? Understandably, they would be extremely appalled that someone would be bold enough to make that statement about their child, and they would feel as if that person was being deliberately critical, disrespectful, cruel, and degrading towards them. And while most Mainstream Parents would find this behavior reprehensible, many of them have no problems rudely asking us Special Needs Parents about our children, their Diagnosis and limitations, and what we are doing to "fix" them.

Please be reminded that we are people too, and we deserve the same level of respect that you rightfully expect us to show you and your child. If a person voluntarily tells you about their child's Diagnosis and limited abilities, then that's okay. That means they feel comfortable sharing that information with you. If they do not volunteer the information, then that means they have decided, for whatever reason, not to discuss it with you at that time.

I fully understand we live in a world that likes to understand the 'why.' People want to know what happened to our children. How did they become Autistic or have other Special Needs? When you ask parents about the 'why,' you are putting them in a situation of having to face the reality of their child's Diagnosis. They may not be mentally prepared to process those unexpected feelings in that time and in that setting.

Every time you ask the 'why' question, you are reminding us of our child's Diagnosis and the difficult things they must face daily. For some, this can lead to feelings of hopelessness and depression. Many Special Needs Parents are already holding on by a thread, and your unexpected 'why' question may force them to go into a state of mind of which they are not prepared to handle in that moment.

Please understand, everyone deals with their child's Diagnosis differently. And that's okay. I mentioned previously that for my peace of mind, and for the betterment of Caleb, I decided not to focus on the 'why' but to rather focus on the 'what'. What I could do from that point forward to help secure a better future and independent life for him. That doesn't mean the 'why' question didn't enter my mind, but I just chose not to allow it to linger there. So, asking me repeatedly why Caleb was diagnosed with Autism, what caused it, and what I am going to do about it, only adds to the level of stress and pressure I already deal with daily.

Please accept the fact that there are questions for which we have no answers. If you asked me how long Caleb was going to be in speech therapy, I would say *'I don't know.'* For the Mainstream Person asking the question, it sounds like it should be a simple answer; but the answer is usually more complex and is based on multiple factors – Are you paying out of pocket for these services?; is your child showing any progress from these services?; how long will you wait to see if the therapy is effective?; does your child have a good rapport with the therapists?; are you able to get your child to the therapy sessions on a regular basis? These are just some of the factors we would have to consider before even beginning to try to answer your question.

Please know it is always our hope that our children will one day have a breakthrough and will 'get it.' So, for most Special Needs Parents, the thought is, the longer our children stay in therapy and work on their skills, the greater the chance a breakthrough will happen for them. Since we have no way of knowing if or when that day will come, many of us want our children to continue therapy for as long as possible. Therefore, when asked how long Caleb would be going to therapy, I can legitimately say, *'I have no idea.'*

ADVICE TO MAINSTREAM: "Our Special Needs Community is Important"

As a Special Needs Parent, we understand you will likely not be able to comprehend most of the things that happen in our daily lives, and we do not hold that against you. There may be times things are going on with our children that we cannot share with you, but we can share with other Special Needs Parents. It's not that we are trying to be standoffish or evasive, but rather some of the things our children do or experience may seem strange to the Mainstream. If I said Caleb likes to wiggle people's

elbows, that would sound strange to a Mainstream Person. If I said it to a Special Needs Parent, they would most likely have a child who has done the same thing or something similar.

Having the support of our Special Needs Community is in no way a means of isolating the Mainstream, but rather provides us with a safe place to go and vent, ask for prayers and support, ask for advice, and receive compassion and understanding. When we interact with this community, we know we are dealing with those who truly understand our lives and various situations, because they are experiencing many of the same things.

Those who are in our Special Needs Community understand we parents do not feel like we are being punished or have done something wrong because we have children with Special Needs. They understand we are all doing our best to take care of our children, and most do not judge. Having that support is invaluable. It helps us to be calmer and more centered, to maintain our sanity, and to be better able to deal with our Mainstream Friends and Family, who don't always understand what we are going through.

CHAPTER SEVEN
"WORDS OF ADVICE FOR THE NEWLY DIAGNOSED"

For Parents who have a child that was recently Diagnosed with Autism or any Special Needs, and you have no idea where to start in helping them; or for those of you who have recently begun the Journey and feel like you have insurmountable obstacles before you; my advice to you is this, First, take a Deep Breath!

I totally understand how scared and overwhelmed you must feel right now, and probably a bit helpless too. I understand how you are anxious to make sure your child gets the help that they need. I also understand how you might be feeling a bit of panic and sense of urgency in wanting to get your child's services started as quickly as possible. Please know that everything will come together!

I would like to offer you some advice on the things I've learned thus far while walking this Autism Journey with My Caleb. I hope it will provide you with some insight and strategies to help you create the best life possible for your child. I hope my recommendations allow you to find some approaches you should take and pitfalls you should avoid.

ADVICE FOR NEWLY DIAGNOSED: "Deal with the Diagnosis Head On"

No matter how hard it is, you must deal with your child's Diagnosis head on. Cry if you must… Scream! Yell! Have a Pity Party! Do whatever you have to do to get it all out. It is important that you deal with those feelings and not pretend like they don't exist. Keeping them bottled up inside and staying in a state of denial may provide some comfort to you, but in the long run it will be totally detrimental to your child. Their quality of life and future depends on you processing those feelings.

It is okay for you to go 'there' and feel those feelings, but you cannot remain there. Sooner than later, you are going to have to wipe the tears off your face, put your shoulders back, roll up your sleeves, and go to work for your child. Their quality of life and future depends on it.

ADVICE FOR NEWLY DIAGNOSED: "It's a Marathon Not a Sprint"

One of the first pieces of advice I received after Caleb's Diagnosis was, this Journey is a marathon and not a sprint. I have to say, after getting the bombshell news of Caleb's Diagnosis, this was the last thing I wanted to hear! To me, they were saying, *'Your child has this Disability Diagnoses, and it's going to take a long time for him to learn and grow.'* Hearing this advice at that time was too much to bear. I remember thinking, *'Oh Okay'* in my head, in response to what they said, but not really believing it in my heart.

While these families had all been walking this Autism Journey for a while, I just didn't want to believe what they were telling me was true. I didn't want to believe it would take a long time for things to get better for Caleb. My mind couldn't comprehend that information. For me to accept those words at that time, made me feel like all hope was lost. It made me feel like I had nothing to hold on to because I just wanted Caleb to learn and grow quick fast and in a hurry!

After walking this Journey for a few years, I came to realize what they said was true. It was very disheartening to accept this fact because a part of me felt sad and overwhelmed at the thought that it might take years for Caleb's learning and skills to get better if it happened at all. I had to learn how to live with the fact that he might not be able to learn beyond a certain point. I had to learn how to be okay with this possibility, while still being optimistic about his future.

Even after all these years, I still find myself from time-to-time wanting to sprint through this Journey with Caleb, and for him to 'hurry up' and learn new skills. I feel that sense of urgency because I'm faced with the fact that he is getting older. When I think about how he has been working on some of the same skills for years, I get discouraged because it seems he may take many more years to learn them.

I am constantly mindful of the passing of time. Caleb is getting older and so am I. I want him to hurry up and learn because I know I won't always be here. But, trying to make this Journey a sprint when it is really a marathon does not in any way change your child's learning and progress, it just creates unnecessary stress and pressure for you. It makes you more tired and worn out. Like me, you must constantly remind yourself to slow down, take things as they come, and to just know in your heart that your child's pace of learning is exactly where it needs to be. And if they are trying, learning is always taking place.

So, I will tell you this again: This Journey will not be a sprint. It will be a marathon and a new way of life. It may take you some time to embrace this concept, and that's okay. I am a firm believer in GOD'S Restorative Power, and I pray for that daily for Caleb. I pray that GOD will give us the knowledge and the know-how to better understand Caleb, his special needs, and how he learns. I also ask GOD to give me the skills and strategies I need to teach Caleb how to communicate and function in this world. I believe there is a right 'formula' of learning for each of our children, and that with its discovery, they can live full and productive lives despite their Diagnosis.

Now, take a deep breath and realize your Child's Diagnosis is not an automatic sentence for a dismal life. With therapy and 1-1 learning time, they may end up adjusting and growing and being able to live a productive life even with their Diagnosis. I have seen it happen many times. This change may happen soon with your child; it may take a long time to happen with your child; or it might not happen at all. Either way, you must never give up hope and always believe that change and growth will happen for them! Regardless of the level of change or the kind of change, you must always remember that any change and progress they make is good!

ADVICE FOR NEWLY DIAGNOSED: "You Are Their Advocate and Their Voice"

You are now your Child's ADVOCATE. You are their VOICE. Don't allow your mind to become so preoccupied with wondering what happened to your child and why they received the Diagnosis. Doing so is a trap to keep you overwhelmed, upset, depressed and in a state of hopelessness about your child's future. Choose, instead, to focus not on the *Why*, but on the *How*.

Always ask yourself, *'How* can I make things better for my child? *How* can I better prepare them for this world and through what services? *How* can I make life better for them?' These are all questions that will move you to action to get things done for your child and will keep you from falling into a state of stagnation and despair. As you are moved to action and are looking for ways to make life better for your child, you will find yourself growing in confidence in being able to advocate for them and to be their voice.

Sadly, there are many people in this world who want to mistreat our children, take advantage of them, and withhold the services they are rightfully and legally entitled to, to function in this world. Therefore, it is important for you to educate yourself on Disability and Discrimination Laws, so when you are in a situation where your child's rights are being violated, you will be readily able to speak up and fight on their behalf. You will be able to hold others accountable for not doing the things they require, and for not prioritizing their needs and services.

By nature, I am a happy-go-lucky, easy-going person. I have an agreeable personality, I typically don't like confrontation, and I am always open to negotiation and trying to make sure everyone feels heard and valued. When it comes to people mistreating Caleb, withholding services, not following his IEP, violating his federal rights, dismissing him, or not giving him the things he needs and is entitled to, you will see a completely different side of me. I DO NOT PLAY WHEN IT COMES TO MY CHILD!

When there is a problem, I will first start at the respective level of where the issues are occurring. I will work my way up from there for as high as I need to go, until it is resolved, and Caleb gets what he needs! I am not asking for anything he is not supposed to have and is rightfully his. I will never allow anyone to do anything that could put Caleb in harm's way nor could break his spirit. I speak for him, and I fight for him. And in doing so, I advocate not only for him, but for all of those in our Special Needs Community. Again, this tenacity and fire is not a part of my regular personality. It is usually hidden as I go about my daily life. But when it comes to Caleb needing Advocacy and a Voice, everyone who is not honoring the things that are rightfully his, will hear my voice, loud and clear!

Not only are you your Child's Advocate and Voice, but one for the entire Special Needs Community as well. Whatever victories you get when fighting for your child, they ultimately benefit all our children. If you find there is a service or program that your child needs that does not exist, step into that Advocate role and talk to your city leaders, teachers, administrators, and all others who are involved. Ask them what it would take to make that change happen. Don't be afraid to speak up and use your voice! I have done these things many times. Sometimes I can get exactly what I am asking for, while other times it might be a modified version. Either way, My Caleb, and our Special Needs Children get something that can help make life better for them.

If you notice something is not right with your child, but you are not exactly sure what it is, ask questions of those involved with them. Be relentless in your pursuit to find the truth! If something is going on at school, talk to their teachers and the administrators. Your child may not be able to verbally tell you what is going on, but they are counting on you to find out what it is and to fix it for them. They are counting on you to speak up and demand they be treated fairly and get the services they need. Even if you feel like you don't have the boldness or courage to speak up, you will find it hidden deep inside you when it comes to your child. Your unending love for them, and your desire to see them have the best life possible, will be all the fuel you need to get out there and fight!

ADVICE FOR NEWLY DIAGNOSED: "Be Willing to Change Your Approach and Think Outside the Box"

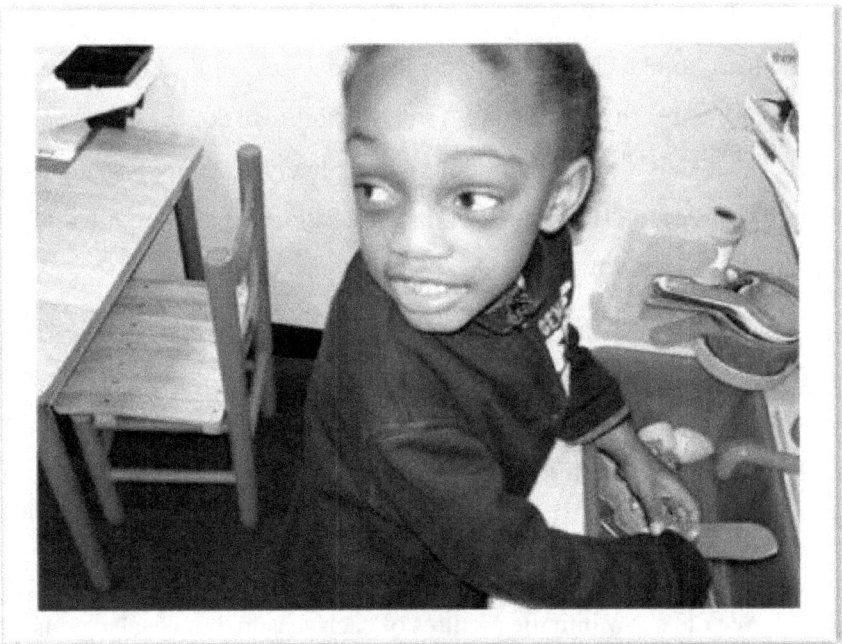

It took me quite a while to shift my mindset about the way Caleb should be learning, especially when it comes to his education. When we were teaching him how to write his name, he would always write the letter "E" with the three short lines going across first, and then he would connect them with the big line going down. I had never seen anyone write an "E" that way. We were always taught to put the big line going down first, and then the three shorter lines across the top, in the middle, and at the bottom.

As he continued to do this, and I kept trying to get him to do it the "right" way, his OT (Occupational Therapist) Ms. Clark finally told me she doesn't correct him on those things. She said if he is writing the letter, that's all that matters. That statement was a true eye-opener for me and the beginning of the change in my thought process about Caleb's learning.

Ms. Clark was right! What difference did it make in the order in which Caleb wrote the letter, so long as it was an "E" when he was done? So many times, we put added pressure on our Special Needs Children to do and learn things the same way as their Mainstream Peers, and we end up measuring their learning success by their ability to do so. I had to accept the fact that Caleb's brain works in a completely different way than his Mainstream Peers. Once I did that, it started to make sense to me that his learning style would be different also.

After this realization, I discovered Caleb's unique learning style. From that point forward, his knowledge began to grow! When his teachers and I wanted him to learn about the weather and seasons and the proper clothing to wear, showing him a picture of the sun and the wind, a coat, and some shorts, meant absolutely nothing to him. So, we took an unconventional approach.

We did show him the pictures of each season, but we also coupled them with a YouTube video showing the weather in action. For in-home learning, I also used a fan to simulate wind, ice to simulate cold, and a heat lamp to simulate heat. Caleb needed to not only see, but 'feel' the differences. In addition, I had a pair of his summer and winter clothes, a coat, and an umbrella (for raining) nearby as we were learning about the seasons so he could better understand what to wear during those times. We did lessons outside in the elements (And yes! Even during those rare times when we got Texas Snow!) to help him make that connection as well!

Because we don't have distinct seasons here in Texas, Caleb's teachers and I chose to focus on summer and heat (which is very similar to spring and fall here), and winter, which of course is cold. While rain is primarily during the spring, we know it can happen at any time. The main thing Caleb needed to know was if it's raining outside, you need an umbrella.

During my newfound quest to think differently about Caleb's learning, I discovered he learns very well through music and song. I created a simple song using mini drums on what the weather and seasons were like, and what he should wear.

"In the summer Caleb!
When it's Hot Outside!
We wear t-shirts and shorts!
We wear t-shirts and shorts!
In the winter Caleb!
When it's Cold Outside!
We wear Sweater! Pants! and Coat!
Sweater! Pants and Coat!
When it's Raining Outside! When It's Raining Outside!
We use an Umbrella! We use an Umbrella!"

During Caleb's learning time, as soon as I or his teacher started beating those drums, it got his attention. He would start smiling and singing along with us, waiting to insert the right words at the right time. His teachers and I made this a part of his learning sessions for an entire school year, both at home and in the classroom. As he and I went throughout our day, when it was windy, cold, hot, or raining outside, I would sing the song and ask him what he would wear, and he would respond! He remembers these things to this day.

Not only did I pattern his learning this way, but I also arranged his drawers in the same manner for each season. During the summer and hotter months, his first drawer holds his t-shirts and the second one holds his shorts. During the winter, his first drawer holds his sweaters and long-sleeved shirts. His second drawer holds his pants. This arrangement reiterates his learning and allows him to choose his clothes in the same order of the song. It provided an excellent structure for Caleb to get his clothes out of his drawers on his own as well without my assistance.

Not only did Caleb learn his weather and seasons and what to wear through song, he also learned how to spell his name. I made up a simple song to the BINGO tune.

"There was a Mommy who had a little boy
And, Caleb was his name Oh!
C-A-L-E-B! C-A-L-E-B! C-A-L-E-B!
And, Caleb was his name Oh!"

I made up songs for him to say his full name when asked, to learn about animals, community helpers, and so much more. It worked every time! If I hadn't opened my mind to the possibility that Caleb learns differently, and just focused on the fact that our methods went against the Mainstream Teaching model, he would have missed learning all these key things.

I'm trying to inspire you to open your mind also and realize first, your child can learn. Watch them closely. See how they respond to the things you are trying to teach them. Is it enough for them to just see a picture of the object or person? Do they also need to 'touch' it? (I found some very realistic animals and community helpers' figurines that we used along with Caleb's pictures and curriculum); do they also need to see it in person? (We took many trips to the zoo to take pictures of Caleb with the animals to incorporate them in his lessons). The point is, it's okay to be as creative as you want to be to meet your child's learning needs and style.

The second point I want to make is, it's okay if your child's learning looks different from their Mainstream Peers. So many times, we spend years trying to fit our Special Needs Children's learning as a square peg into a round hole. No matter how many times we try, nor how many options we explore, if something doesn't fit, it never will.

Case in point, Caleb's learning to read was a personal goal that was very important to me. When I looked at his abilities from a Mainstream Perspective, learning to read seemed impossible. A fellow Special Needs Parent introduced me to PCI, a new reading program. It was not based on the traditional, phonetic, sounding-out-the-words way we learned in school, but rather it was a new program that taught reading through the use of repeated words and recognition.

When we started using this new program, Caleb utterly amazed me when he was not only recognizing the words but was reading them! He was moving from one book to the next in their series of books! I can't even adequately express the Joy that was in my heart to see that the ability for him to read was there! Had I tried to continue to pursue the traditional model of learning to read, we would have never discovered Caleb had this skill. Our children are so full of hidden treasures! We just have to meet them where they are and stop waiting and expecting them to conform to our ideas on how learning should take place.

Once I started down this new learning path., I shared my ideas with Caleb's teachers, and they all got on board. They too, started looking for new ways to teach him. We all saw how Caleb enjoyed his learning even more. During his sessions, we were able to get more 1-1 focused learning time, and it was an even greater learning experience for all involved.

ADVICE FOR NEWLY DIAGNOSED: "Use the Partnership Approach"

It's interesting because most of my closest friends are Caleb's former teachers and therapists. Not only are they intent on staying connected with Caleb (us) after he moves on from them, but we want to stay connected to them as well. It is important to me that they can follow Caleb's Journey and progress so they can see their efforts in working with him were fruitful and not in vain. And they can see firsthand the differences they made in his life.

I encourage you, no matter what role the people involved play in your child's life, to first focus on building relationships. Whether someone will be teaching your child for one school year or more; or a bus driver will be dropping your child off; or your child will be attending therapy twice a week; I feel it is important to build relationships with the people working with and interacting with your child for an extended period. The more you communicate with them, the better aligned you can be in making sure your child is getting the help and services they need. It also allows you to readily share with each other any behaviors and occurrences that happened in the classroom, in therapy, and at home. You can then share ideas and techniques that worked (or not) in each of the respective settings.

Utilizing this approach also ensures Caleb's learning is unilateral. Whether he be at home, in the classroom, at therapy, or out in the community, we are all speaking the same language, doing the same things, and setting the same expectations. This approach allows Caleb to have a clearer understanding of what he should be doing and how he should be responding, regardless of who is working with him at that time.

ADVICE FOR NEWLY DIAGNOSED: "Use Your Parental Power in Your Child's Education"

Regardless of your child's Disability, one of the most important things you must do is become fully informed of their Educational Rights! Our Special Needs Children's learning is protected under federal law. The school is mandated to meet their Special Needs to make sure they are provided a Free and Appropriate Public Education (FAPE) just like their Mainstream Peers. The law does not allow the school to discriminate against or withhold services from our children in any way because of their Disability.

Irrespective of their ability to learn, our children should be given the same learning opportunities as their Mainstream Peers. They should have educational goals set up for them annually through an Individualized Education Program (IEP) that is solidified in an annual ARD (Arrival, Review, Dismissal) meeting; and their teachers are required to work with them 1-1 on their goals throughout the year on a consistent and measurable basis.

In most cases, most of our children need an extended period beyond a year to carry out their learning goals. The teacher is not penalized if the student does not meet their goals within a one-year period; they are, however, required to track the student's progress via the system and show proof that they did work with them on their goals.

The federal government also mandates that our children receive the necessary tools and accommodations they need to help them while working on their goals. For example, an accommodation for a student who is visually impaired may be an over-sized monitor to help them to better see their learning materials. Or it may be determined that a child with Autism might benefit from using a weighted lap throw when doing their assignments to help keep them calm.

Most of the accommodations are based on recommendations from teachers, speech, and occupational therapists, and from parental input. Once the accommodations are made an official part of the student's IEP Goals, the choice to use them is no longer optional. Every teacher or person involved in the student's learning must use these accommodations. Delivering anything less for our students is against federal law.

Your Student's IEP is a legal-binding document. The teachers cannot deviate from the agreed upon goals in the Plan; they must measure, track, and document the student's progress in working on their goals; and the IEP cannot be changed at any time without a new official ARD (Admission Review Dismissal) Meeting being held, including the parent and all other relevant professionals involved.

At that time, new discussions on the student's learning will take place; decisions will be made on what things need to be added or taken away in the IEP; a new IEP Document is created, and the teachers, campus, therapist, and district are all accountable to follow the Plan as written. It is not open for interpretation.

As a parent, it is your job to watch your child's learning and IEP to make sure it is being followed, and the progress-tracking is taking place. If it is not, you need to intervene at once and hold those accountable for not doing their jobs. One of the ways you can do this is by making sure you receive your child's 9-week progress report. At the very least, it should have a 'grade' for your child in each area of their goals. Some may also have their progress-tracking information and the number of attempts they made while working on their goals. You can also email or speak with your child's teacher periodically to ask how they are doing, and/or set up a meeting with them during their Conference Period. Just because our children have Special Needs doesn't mean it is not important for you to be directly involved in their education.

It has always been my practice to meet with all of Caleb's teachers and therapists before his ARD to help establish his IEP goals. I like this approach because first, it allows me to give input on the things I feel are important for Caleb to work on during the school year, and it helps me to know what things he will be focusing on for the year in the classroom. Knowing his goals allows me to better track his progress when I have my progress meetings with his teachers. Knowing Caleb's goals also helps me to know what I should be working with him on at home to reinforce his learning at school.

Secondly, I find this approach to be valuable because most ARDs are hard! Even with everyone in the room coming into agreement before the meeting starts (based on your meeting with them 1-1 beforehand), you as a parent still must sit there and listen to an hour-long meeting, hearing everyone in the room discussing your child's deficiencies, and telling you what they cannot do. It is a very emotionally taxing meeting. Those involved are not trying to be deliberately cruel. They just must give a realistic account of their expert view on your child's abilities to learn. These assessments are necessary to ensure your child gets all the services and accommodations they need.

Even in knowing this, the meetings are still hard. I have yet to not cry after I've left one. That's why, if you take the time to meet with everyone 1-1 before the ARD meeting, you can come to an agreement on what your child's goals will be (rather than hashing it out in a much longer

ARD meeting), and the time spent in the meeting will be just a matter of going through the formalities.

As previously mentioned, it is imperative that you educate yourself on your child's educational rights! If you do not, you will find some teachers, administrators, and school districts will do the bare minimum to facilitate your child's learning. Some will have them sitting in a classroom all day doing nothing. This is unacceptable! There are many Special Needs and Autism Groups on social media that address a variety of issues, including educational ones. It is crucial that you connect with your fellow Special Needs Community members, ask questions, share your stories; and, if needed, hire an Advocate to join you in ARD meetings to represent your child and speak on their behalf.

As a parent, you are a strong voice for your child. Use it when you need it! I love taking the Partnership Approach with Caleb's teachers and administrators to try and work out any differences or concerns. On the occasions when issues arise, I've found most involved are eager to sit down to discuss the matter and find a resolution. If, for some reason that is not the case, I always choose to follow the chain of command when moving forward. I want to always give every person at each level the opportunity to fix the problem. If that does not happen, I will keep escalating upward for as far as I need to go.

When dealing with any issues or concerns in your child's learning and education, it is important that you document every encounter you have with all involved. This documentation also includes making learning requests on behalf of your child. Even if you have a conversation with someone in person, you should still follow it up with an email outlining when and where the discussion took place, (e.g., 'I spoke with you this morning at the drop-off about..'), what was discussed when you spoke with them, what your concerns are, and the next steps on how you would like to see them addressed and/or resolved. This documentation creates a paper trail to confirm the proper person was notified should you need it later.

While no district is perfect, Caleb and I have been fortunate enough to be in a great one, in Grand Prairie ISD. It has a strong, progressive, Special Education Program. I'm sure my robust parental involvement in helping to establish Caleb's goals; scheduling meetings with his teachers and therapists periodically throughout the year to discuss his progress; strong advocacy for Caleb, his classmates, and even his teachers; and continued concerted efforts to connect with Caleb's teachers to build strong relationships, have helped make his learning process a greater success.

Always remember, when your child walks into their classroom, they cannot speak for themselves. They are relying on you to do it for them. And nine-times-out-of-ten, if they can't tell you something is wrong, you will know it by a change in their behavior. It is always the number one tell-tell sign!

ADVICE FOR NEWLY DIAGNOSED: "Get Them Out There and Involved"

When Caleb was born, he showed no signs of Autism. We got him out in the community regularly just like any of his Mainstream Peers. At the point when he received his Diagnosis, he was already used to going out in public. It helped him to deal with sensory issues.

As more of his Autism behaviors began to show, I found myself hesitating to take him out as much in public. My main concern was him having a meltdown. Out of all the Autism behaviors I had to deal with in the beginning, meltdowns were my biggest nightmare and fear. Therefore, it would have been easier for me to not take Caleb out in public places and just keep him at home. I had to fight hard against this temptation. I first had to get to the point where I stopped caring about what people thought.

I then had to make sure I always had a plan. While nothing is foolproof, I maintained control over any potential situation as much as I could.

When attending indoor events, I made sure we were always sitting on the outskirts of a room, near an easy exit; or if we were at an outdoor function, we sat at the very back away from the main crowd. I made sure I had all of Caleb's necessities, (his favorite cup/toy/a go-to bag), and a change of clothes. I made sure we were always prepared to leave at a moment's notice. And I watched Caleb like a hawk to observe his behaviors, actions, reactions, and his facial expressions, to monitor any changes in his mood. In time, I was able to read Caleb so much, I could usually tell when something was about to happen, and it was time to go.

For those occasions, however, where I couldn't prevent something from happening, I just ignored the people around me and dealt with the situation as best I could in the moment. If something out of the ordinary happened (e.g., he bumped into someone or ran into a group of people uncontrollably), and I felt the need to announce to those around us, *'He had Autism'* I would do so. Most people were empathetic and understanding. However, if I didn't feel the need to announce the Autism, I wouldn't.

Yes, it would have been easier to avoid those situations by keeping Caleb home, but had I done that, he would never have learned how to be in a setting with other people, surrounded by different noises, and multiple things happening around him. Being out among people also teaches Caleb there are other kinds of people in this world who are going to be doing a variety of things. Caleb needs to be exposed to their comings-and-goings and happenings to realize the real world is not as organized and structured as we try to make his to be.

The more we got Caleb out into the world, the more he became accustomed to being in it. That doesn't mean he has perfected being out in public and never has any issues, and I am not still watching him like a hawk to make sure he is okay. It's just now he is more accustomed to these outings and has a better idea of what to expect.

Even when Caleb doesn't have meltdowns when we are out, he is very likely at some point to let out a few unexpected yelps or start his happy swaying and sing-song'ing. During these times, I have gotten to the point where I just let him be himself. I used to get stressed out trying to keep Caleb quiet and calm and to not draw any attention to himself. But then I realized, we readily accept younger Mainstream Children being loud and playful and making their cute noises when they are out. Our Special Needs Children, regardless of their age, should be able to do the same. They shouldn't have to minimize or hide who they are just to appease those around them.

Not only is it a good idea to get your child out in the community, but it is also an opportunity for you to support the businesses and organizations that provide Special Events just for our community. As much as Caleb and I can, we always try to go to places like Studio Movie Grill who provides Special Screenings just for our children and families; the many Water Parks who designate days and times for our children and families to come out and enjoy the park without all the crowds; Chuck-E-Cheese, and various Trampoline Parks that have designated times for our children to play unencumbered, and so many more!

It's great to be able to take our children to these events where they can totally be themselves, and we parents do not have to deal with the added stress of monitoring their behavior and actions, while amongst their Mainstream Peers. The more we support activities like these, the more organizers will see our appreciation for their services and will be encouraged to continue providing them.

Another reason why it is good to get our children out in the community is, Mainstream Society needs to be reminded that our Special Needs Children and Community are part of our greater society. Seeing our children is a reminder to them that our world is made up of people from all ages, stages, ethnicities, races, and abilities. It is also a reminder that the Mainstream must learn to live with these diversities, even if they sadly, don't always accept them.

ADVICE FOR NEWLY DIAGNOSED: "Challenge Your Children. They Will Surprise You."

As much as I used to say there wasn't anything Caleb couldn't do, I realized after he joined Special Olympics, I was holding on to some limitations in my mind. When his then coach and my dear friend Pam Fowler said she wanted him to participate in basketball, bowling and track and field, my first thought was, *'He can't do that.'* I felt that way because I immediately thought about Caleb doing those activities in the traditional way. Based on that thought, I was right. He wouldn't be able to do it. When she started working with Caleb, however, and showed me there were alternative ways to participate in sports, my mind was completely opened!

When Coach Pam mentioned Caleb taking part in basketball, I immediately thought of the team sport. I thought there was no way he could learn plays, shooting, when to play defense, etc. I didn't realize she was referring to basketball skills. Special Olympics has the basketball team sport competition, and they also have basketball skills for those who are unable to or are not interested in playing on a team.

When Coach Pam started working with Caleb, showing him how to dribble, shoot through hula hoops, and do bounce passes against the wall, He Did It! I was stunned! I felt the greatest sense of pride, and the lowest shame, all at the same time. I felt great pride that he could do something new that I never imagined, and shame that I never even considered he could do so.

I experienced the exact same scenario when it was time for Caleb to participate in bowling and track and field. Coach Pam said she thought Caleb could do it and I doubted it. I later realized I had little faith in Caleb's ability to do these things, because I was only thinking of him competing in the traditional sense. After much practice, Caleb became an avid bowler, using a ramp and not the bumpers; and he went from being able to run in any lane during the 50-yard-dash, to being able to stay in his lane for the entire race.

Seeing all the amazing things Caleb could do caused me to see him in a completely different light. Every time I wanted him to try something, and my mind automatically told me he couldn't do it, I pushed past that thought to have him try it anyways. Caleb has amazed me by being able to roller skate with no lessons; he went up in a small engine plane with me (for a Special Needs excursion) even though he had never flown before; he did rock climbing even though he's never had any training; he's played Miracle League Baseball for years and has learned how to bat on his own and run the bases; he's been able to not only go to Special Needs Movie Screenings but to the regular movies as well; he did indoor sky-diving with me; he creates beautiful paintings, he sings songs with me; and so much more!

When I found out our district had a Special Education Department Talent Show, I wanted Caleb to take part. He had never been on a stage nor had performed in front of a crowd, but I still wanted him to try. The first year, he blew me away when he got on stage, (I stood up there with him for support), and without hesitation he started playing his full-sized keyboard, manipulating the various sounds and beats. He was rocking back and forth, smiling, and jumping around. It was as if he had done it a hundred times before. He showed no fear!

For every year thereafter, he's participated in the Talent Show regularly. He sang a song with me, we did a hip hop dance, a tap dance, and he participated in a dance with his fellow classmates. His wonderful Special Olympics Peer Partner, Chris, was always there as part of our Group, "Caleb and the Crowdettes." We had a Blast! Had I not allowed my mind to be open to new possibilities and the things Caleb could do, I would have never known all those wonderful things were inside of him.

ADVICE FOR NEWLY DIAGNOSED: "Create A Safe, Thriving, Environment for Them."

When Caleb was first Diagnosed, I tried to do everything I could to maintain a traditional home as everyone expected. Not only was I dealing with the stress of raising a child with Autism, but also from trying to maintain the façade of how everyone thought we should be living. Thankfully, I finally got to the place where I realized in order to have a life that was manageable, I had to create an environment that was based on Caleb's Special Needs and not on what others expected.

If Caleb needed to have his special cup with him everywhere he went to help him feel safe and calm, that's what we brought. If Caleb needed to always have his snacks laid out throughout the day, that's what we did. If Caleb felt more comfortable sitting at his desk to eat, rather than at the table, that's what we did. Trying to keep up with Mainstream societal traditions and doing things others felt were right for our lives, only brought about added stress and disharmony; and oftentimes, they disrupted Caleb's surroundings and peace. If Caleb's diet was limited due to sensory issues, and he wanted to have chicken nuggets for breakfast, he was entitled to have what made him feel safe in his world. We made sure he still got the vitamins and minerals he needed. If he wanted to have a certain kind of cover for his bed, or certain toys when he took a bath, we supplied those things because they made his world feel safe.

People will come into your world and tell you how it should be structured and what you should be doing. Don't Allow It! You and your spouse or significant other need to decide what kind of home and environment you want to create for your child and then do it without apology! Your child's peace of mind, feelings of safety and acceptance, and having a sense of well-being and comfort, are the only things that matter. When your child feels that sense of safety and security at home, it allows them to be able to learn and grow and adapt more quickly to their outside surroundings. It gives them a feeling of reassurance in knowing that regardless of what happens outside the home, they always have a safe and familiar place to return to.

ADVICE FOR NEWLY DIAGNOSED: "Extend Grace to Fellow Special Needs Parents"

I recently saw a social media post from a mom in one of our social media Special Needs Groups. She had posted an open birthday invitation for her child's birthday party which was more than a month away. She was upset about the fact that few people had responded that they were coming. Seeing that post prompted me to write this section.

We, as Special Needs Parents must extend grace to our fellow Special Needs Families. We can't just assume if someone does not support our endeavors, they do not care about what is happening with our children and families and should be reprimanded.

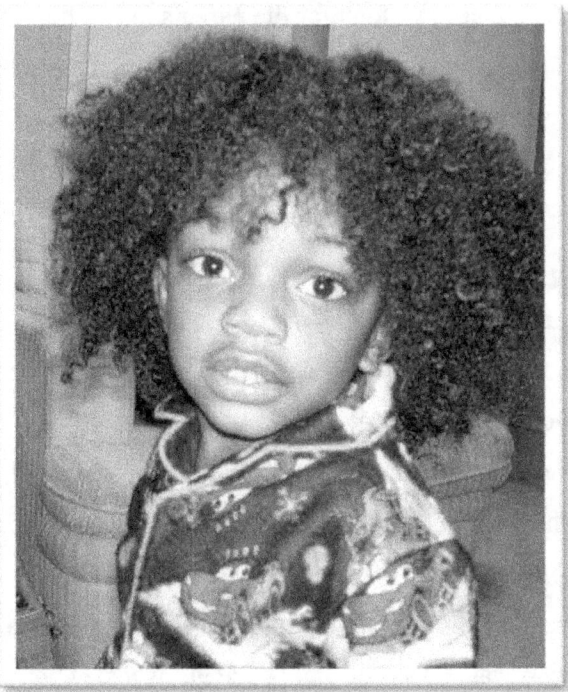

This original poster was upset about the fact that people were saying they couldn't come. I thought their responses were a courteous gesture because they didn't leave her dangling at the last minute, wondering if anyone would show up. She was also upset that some people hadn't yet responded. The event was more than a month away. I know in many cases, I wouldn't even have been able to respond to something that far in advance. This may have been the reasons others hadn't responded yet either.

The bottom line is, it's not fair to put unnecessary stress and pressure on those who already have so much of it on them. In situations such as this one, we not only have to extend grace to our fellow Special Needs Families but be willing to accept the outcome whether it means one child can come or twenty children can come. We must decide we are going to be happy with the fact that at least some were able to make it, and we must recognize the effort it took for the parents to get their children there. I used the birthday party as an example, but there are many instances where we must make sure we are looking at things from the right perspective and are appreciative of other's efforts.

There was an occasion where a fellow Autism Mom, and a very good friend of mine named Jennifer invited Caleb and I to come to her daughter's birthday party. She lives about an hour away. I responded 'Yes', we would go, and when I did, I had every intention of honoring my word. As time got closer to the event, however, I was feeling more and more exhausted. Caleb was having some major issues at school with multiple teachers and medication changes, and his reactions to an overall terrible lack of structure in the classroom.

As we neared the end of the week, I knew as much as I wanted to go to the party, I was exhausted and needed to just stay home and rest. A few days before the event, I reached out to Jenniefer and told her regrettably we would not be able to come. It was the hardest thing for me to do because I always like to honor my commitments, and I knew how much she and I were looking forward to seeing each other again.

When I reached out to her, I braced myself for her response. Even though she is the sweetest person in the world, and a harsh response from her would have been out of character, I still didn't know what her reaction would be. I expected her to be very disappointed and upset with me. She didn't respond unkindly at all. She simply said she understood and told me to rest. She didn't just say it, she absolutely meant it.

While I still felt terrible about us not being able to go, and like I was letting her down, she repeatedly told me it was okay. She said she understood I was tired and getting my rest was more important than anything else. I can't even put into words how much her understanding and sincere response meant to me. It touched my heart so deeply and brought tears to my eyes.

So, when I saw the social media post from one of our fellow Special Needs Moms, I was reminded that Jennifer didn't try to make me feel guilty or outcasted. She made me feel okay with choosing to value myself first above all else, and to get the rest that I desperately needed. If you find yourself in a situation where you feel a fellow Special Needs Mom or Parent has let you down, please consider these things: she might have had her roughest week yet with her child; she might be running on fumes and a few hours of sleep; she might be dealing with major changes in her child, in the household, or both; she may just be at the end of her rope.

I shared this information with you not as an attempt to judge the fellow Special Needs Mom for her post and response, but rather to help you to realize there are always extenuating circumstances in every situation. While we fellow Special Needs Parents may not share with each other all the reasons why we can't come to an event, let's just consider something that has occurred and give each other the benefit of the doubt. Many times, we unfairly expect our fellow Special Needs Families to go above and beyond to support us because we understand each other's lives and the rejections we experience. While it is good for us to look to each other for support, we must still remember we are all living our lives and are doing the best we can to manage our own daily challenges.

ADVICE FOR NEWLY DIAGNOSED: "You Design Your Life Not Others"

I have said many times your lives are going to change. Many reading this will still try to do everything they can to pattern their lives after the Mainstream. That is up to you. For me, it just created an added layer of stress that I finally decided I didn't need.

For the first few years after Caleb's Diagnosis, Curtis and I tried to continue doing all the things our Mainstream Friends and Family members did. One of the areas in which it was the hardest for us to keep up with was family and friends' outings and special events. When something was planned, everyone expected us to all three come, Curtis, Caleb, and me. They not only expected us to come, but they also expected us to stay the entire time like everyone else. They expected Curtis and I to spend time with the adults and for Caleb to play with the other children.

They totally dismissed the fact that Caleb had Autism and was dealing with unique behaviors.

While attending these functions, we were never able to go, fully relax, and have a good time like everyone else. Usually, one of us always had to be near Caleb to make sure he was okay, wasn't having a meltdown, wasn't spinning, jumping, or running into everyone, and doing any number of other things. The three of us trying to stay the entire time was also a huge problem. Caleb would let us know in his definite way he was nearing his sensory overload point, but we would still try to stay a little longer because we knew others would get upset if we left early.

And then the following events usually occurred: we would prolong leaving; Caleb would have some sort of outburst or meltdown; friends and family would look at him like he was a terrible, misbehaving child; they would give us parental advice as we were leaving, about how we needed to be 'stricter' with him and his behavior; we would leave feeling ashamed, embarrassed and upset; Caleb would be worn out; and our memories of the evening would not be good ones. This pattern continued repeatedly. Every time we left, we felt like the most inadequate parents, and the looks of disapproval we received from our friends and family made us feel like complete failures.

Finally, Curtis and I decided we were going to do things differently! The next time we were invited to an outing or event, we decided which one of us was going to go, and if we would be taking Caleb. Usually with family outings, we base our decision to go on whoever's side of the family extended the invitation. Curtis would primarily attend with his family, and I with mine. Then, it would just be a matter of whether Caleb would go also or stay home with the other one. When it came to attending other events with friends and in the community, I was usually the one who took Caleb while Curtis either worked or rested. Or I would attend them by myself, and Caleb would stay home with Curtis. The bottom line is, we took back control over our lives and the decision-making process and did what we thought was best for our family at that time.

There have been many times in our new life's structure where we decided not to attend the event or occasion all together. Many of these decisions were not easy, but we felt they were best at the time. Caleb might have been having a hard day already; we might have been up all evening with him the night before; or, we might have both simply been too tired to go. It's not that these decisions are made easily, and we enjoyed disregarding spending time with others. Many times, we might really want to go to an event or outing, but simply know it's not the best decision. Our new life's design now gives us the freedom to be realistic about what is happening in our lives in that moment, and to decide if attending an event or outing will make things better or worse.

As you can imagine, we got a lot of flak and negative talk from friends and family members about us doing things differently. The same people who scolded us about Caleb's behavior when we brought him to the events, were the same ones who scolded us for not bringing him to the events. They also talked about us when only one of us would either show up with Caleb at an event, or one of us would come alone to 'represent' the family. They even called our marriage into question when we didn't come together. There was no winning with them. Consequently, making the decision to finally live our lives and do things the way that was the best suited for our family was the best thing we could have ever done.

People still talk about us, but that's okay. We have learned to deal with it. At the end of the day, we no longer must deal with those exhausting situations of Caleb having sensory overloads while we are trying to be someone others want us to be. We don't get invited to many of those functions anymore, and that's okay.

We find attending events and outings that are geared towards our Special Needs Community much easier and more enjoyable. We don't have to explain Caleb's behavior. He can be himself. He can be around people who understand him. Curtis and I must no longer explain why one of us is out with him and the other one is not; and we don't have the added pressure of trying to fit the mode of how our Mainstream Friends and Family members feel we should be.

Not only are outings and events opportunities for you to design your life in the way that best suits you and your family, but you can also design your life in other areas as well. After posting some pictures of Caleb and I at a fun outing, one of my friends commented that Caleb needed some friends. I'm sure she didn't mean to be crass, but I was taken aback by her comment. People look at Caleb and because they feel he doesn't "look" Disabled, they want to ascribe Mainstream behaviors and labels to him. What she didn't realize was Caleb has friends. She just assumed because he does a lot of things with me, that must mean he doesn't have any friends. He does have friends, and there are occasions when they are able to join us for outings and events. Caleb's relationships with his friends, however, do not look the same as his Mainstream Peers' friendships.

Because I want Caleb to have a full and active life, I have designed our lives around my doing a lot of activities with him. Many times, his friends are not always readily available to do things with him. This way he doesn't miss out on fun events because his Special Needs Friend's Parents are not always able to bring their children. They are all dealing with their own unique family challenges. Since I considered this person to be a dear friend, I chose to just disregard her response as a lack of knowledge of the lives of our Special Needs Children.

One final issue that is near and dear to my heart when encouraging you to design your life, is birthday parties for our children. Countless number of times I have seen stories about Special Needs Parents being devastated because their child invited many people (usually Mainstream Children) to their birthday party, and no one showed up. The thought of this occurring to even one of our children is heartbreaking to me.

It is occurrences like these that caused me to design our lives in such a way that Caleb nor I would ever have to deal with something so traumatizing. Rather than trying to follow the Mainstream and do things the way they would, we decided to create our own Birthday Traditions for Caleb. Doing so eliminated a huge amount of stress and pressure in trying to do things the way others felt they should be done.

For us, instead of scheduling a party for Caleb and trying to get others to come, we choose to take him out to do several of his favorite activities like jumping, skating, and going to the movies over the course of a few days. We also take him out to eat as well. Utilizing this approach has helped to end a lot of the unknowns (if people will come), and it gives us more control over the situation.

Caleb gets to do the things that he enjoys the most, and we know he is going to have a great time. For the occasions when some of his friends are available to join us, I will invite 1-3 of them to come and enjoy his favorite activities with him. I am not telling you to forget scheduling a traditional birthday party for your child if that's what you want to do. As Caleb gets older, we may change course and decide to have a traditional party for him with friends. I'm just trying to point out when choosing to design your life in the way that works best for your family, there are other nontraditional options available.

Once again, I strongly recommend that you design your life and not allow others to define it for you. Your design may look completely different from mine and that is perfectly okay. I shared this information with you to help you see there are many other options out there that might work for you. The most important thing is for you to have the courage to go against the grain and do what is best for you and your family, and to do the things that bring about the most joy and peace for your child.

ADVICE FOR NEWLY DIAGNOSED: "Connecting with Others is Your Lifeline"

Please hear me clearly when I say, this Journey is too vast, this load is too heavy, and these Roads are too unpredictable, for you to try to walk them alone. Should you try to do so, you will squander the strength you desperately need to care for your child. As I am writing this to you, I must keep reminding myself of this very thing as well. You can either try to carry the load alone: because you feel you can do it without any help; or you may do what I do: get so caught up in the Journey that you just do not stop to reach out for help.

Connecting with others reminds you that your life and raising a child with Special Needs is not as unique as you think. It reminds you that there are other families who are going through or have gone through the same things as you. Knowing this keeps you from feeling so isolated and alone when things get hard.

Our Special Needs Community is wonderful. We believe in encouraging and strengthening one another and celebrating each other's successes. There are many Groups on social media to connect with to help you build a strong community of supporters for both you and your child. If you find the kind of support and group you need isn't out there, create one. It costs you nothing to set up a Community Page on social media.

Sadly, you will find most of your key connections and support often does not come from close friends and family members. Many Times, because of their close connections to us, they feel the most entitled to tell us how we should be running our lives and raising our children. Their views are oftentimes tainted because they are trying to deal with us as the person they knew us as before, rather than as the person we are now: a parent with a Special Needs Child. They don't understand we are now different, and our lives are different.

Other Special Needs Parents and Families readily understand the things occurring in our lives when our Mainstream Friends and Family members do not. Sometimes, rather than trying to understand our lives and the things we deal with, our close friends and family members start resenting our new relationships and connections with other Special Needs Families. They try to make us feel guilty about them.

Each of you must decide how you are going to deal with those new relationship dynamics, and whether you are going to keep the ones with those in the Special Needs Communities who support you, versus friends and family who do not. Only you can decide which relationships you want to keep, maintain from a distance, or end altogether.

I have personally decided, NO ONE, friends or family, gets to be in my life and mistreat my child nor me. Our lives are hard enough without that added stress and pressure, and I must reserve all my strength and energy for My Caleb. He deserves my very best.

ADVICE FOR NEWLY DIAGNOSED: "You Don't Have to Prove Anything to Anyone"

For those of you who, like me, came from a corporate background or you were someone who was always actively involved in the community and in the spotlight, this advice is for you. Please know you don't have to try to keep up with all the happenings and attend all the events to show others (or even yourself) that you are still involved and can 'do it all!'

Because I am known for being actively involved in our community, and I came from a corporate background, I felt the need to try and remain connected to everything, while still having the immense energy needed to raise Caleb. I accepted every speaking engagement, took part in every volunteer opportunity, and showed up for every special appearance, whether it served my overall Life's Purpose or not.

I eventually accepted the fact that while I enjoyed many of the things I was doing, many were done because I either didn't want to say 'No', or I was trying to maintain my image. I knew most people gauged my level of 'success' by how involved I was in everything. I didn't want them to think differently of me.

After following this path for many years, and Caleb's Special Needs became more demanding, I realized I had to stop and prioritize the things that were most important. I stopped accepting every invitation that was offered to me, even some that I genuinely wanted to do. I stopped taking part in things that did not support My Life's Purpose of Advocating for and Supporting our Special Needs Children and Community. I even had to carefully consider the things I was asked to do in relation to our Special Needs Community and realized I couldn't always say 'Yes' simply because it was for us. I had to learn to be strategic and specific in my approach.

This change was not easy for me! It did not come overnight. For someone who has a Ministry of Helps and gets so much satisfaction and joy out of helping others, it was hard to say 'No.' My decisions were made through a series of careful thought and consideration of each opportunity presented, and my evaluating where it would fit in my life at that time. I knew it was necessary to make this change because I was spreading myself thin. I was trying to help everyone else and was overwhelmed and exhausted when trying to take care of My Caleb. He was the one who needed me the most.

Making this change showed me very quickly who my 'true' friends and supporters were. Some people are deeply offended when you must tell them 'No,' even when you fully explain your reasons for doing so. This decision may also put you 'outside the crowd' because some people will treat you differently if you are not always at all the happening events. You must be careful not to allow your lack of participation or their lack of invites to events, to define your worth. Don't let it make you feel like a failure; simply because you have decided to stop burning the candle at both ends, doing everything for everybody.

You must also fight that voice inside your head that says you are letting others down. Remind yourself instead, that the only person that matters and deserves your complete, undivided, fully present attention is your Special Needs Child. People are going to think what they want to think about you, and that's okay!

This change will not come overnight. Each time you choose to make meeting your child's needs your number one priority; it will get easier. Eventually, you will find choosing to spend all your energy on meeting their needs first becomes second nature. There will be occasions where you will find taking part in an event might not be possible at one time but may be at another. The bottom line is you get to choose. You get to decide what is best for you and your family, and you are not allowing those around you to make or influence those decisions. The worst thing in the world is having to live with the results of the decisions others have made for you and your family! You're bound and miserable trying to do so, while they are out there living their lives freely.

ADVICE FOR NEWLY DIAGNOSED: "You Can't Share Everything"

Just as it is important for you to connect with others who are also raising Special Needs Children, it is equally important for you to know you can't share everything with some of your Mainstream Friends and Family members. They simply will not understand many of the things that are going on in our world. Their lack of understanding may often lead to judgment and unsolicited advice.

If you told them your 21-year-old child must have his ten stuffed animals in the car with him everywhere he goes, they wouldn't understand. If you told them your 12-year-old daughter likes to sleep on a mattress on the floor because she doesn't like the feeling of being elevated, they wouldn't understand. If you told them your 5-year-old child was being aggressive with you and you were afraid of them, they wouldn't understand.

Those in your Special Needs Groups and Communities would totally understand. Most outside of it, however, would not. Their lack of awareness would just lead to many questions you are likely not able to answer. It doesn't make them bad people. They just simply don't understand our lives and are processing the situation from their Mainstream point of view.

ADVICE FOR NEWLY DIAGNOSED: "Never! Ever! Compare Your Child with Others!"

One of the greatest pieces of advice I can give a parent or person raising a child with Special Needs, is to never, ever, compare them to other children – even those who have the same Diagnosis! When you do this, you will end up wearing yourself out, depleting your hope, and draining all your strength and energy. It will only put you in a perpetual state of disheartedness, misery, and despair.

As a society, we are trained to group and categorize people, and have expectations that everyone within those groups will behave in a certain way. When I saw the quote, *"If you've met one child with Autism, you've met one child"* it really resonated with me. Most of us, when we begin this Journey, develop a perception of how an Autistic or Special Needs Child should be based on what we see on TV, in the movies, stories we've heard, and even from our own experiences when interacting with other Special Needs Children.

While the Diagnosis might be the same, the child is not the same. Our children, just like their Mainstream Peers, are all unique and different individuals. There may be areas where one child is flourishing, and another is lacking. One child may be nonverbal, but highly social; and another child may be verbal and higher functioning but doesn't like to be touched. The reason why it is called the Autism *Spectrum* is because there are so many degrees of strengths and limitations from one end to the other. These degrees of differences are why we must never judge anyone else's Autistic Child's abilities. While your child may not have limitations in the same areas as theirs, your child still has limitations, nonetheless. We are all on the same Journey, just traveling different Roads.

There are times when you may see stories of other Autistic or other Special Needs Children meeting their milestones and doing extraordinary things, and you might find yourself feeling a tug in your heart. On one hand, you feel happy and proud for the family and their child's success; and on the other, you feel sad because a part of you wants your child to have that same success also. It's okay to have these feelings. You can't, however, dwell on them for long because your focus must always be on your child and the things they are accomplishing, whether big or small. If you are so busy comparing your child to other children and reveling in their success, you run the risk of overlooking the wonderful things your child is doing as well.

Each child should be treated with love and respect regardless of where they fall on the Spectrum. Our children should have programs geared towards their personal growth and development, not based on the overall belief of the needs of all children with Autism, collectively. We must meet every child right where they are in their abilities and set realistic expectations for their growth and development. We must not add additional pressure to a child who is already struggling just to survive in a world where most people around them don't understand them.

ADVICE FOR NEWLY DIAGNOSED: "Don't Judge"

Earlier, I recommended to those who do not have Special Needs Children to not judge. Unfortunately, I must also do the same for those who are in our Special Needs Community as well.

Sadly, I have seen Special Needs Parents whose children are excelling in one area, judge their fellow Special Needs Parents whose children are struggling. Either they question the parent's methods of handling the situation; they offer unsolicited advice on how they would (or did) do things differently; or they talk about the parent to others behind their back. Not only is this extremely demeaning, hurtful, and counterproductive, but it is also setting a bad precedence. While your child may not be having any difficulties or struggling in that area at that time, that doesn't mean they might not in the future. None of us knows the challenges our children will face.

When someone else's child is going through a challenging time and we are on the outside looking in, it's easy to judge how the situation is being handled. Caleb went through a time where he was having a major medical issue that involved painful bladder spasms. While I have never had them, the doctor said the pain was so bad it would bring a grown man to his knees. Caleb dealt with these spasms for weeks before they finally figured out what was wrong with him.

When the spasms came, my always sweet, kind, happy, loving little boy would start crying, hitting, grabbing, scratching, flailing his arms and kicking his legs. As we were doing everything we could to address and fix the issue, I learned some of my fellow Special Needs moms were talking about me to others, and about Caleb's behavior. Up until this point in our Journey, I had never experienced anything like this from our Special Needs Community. Even though they knew what Caleb was going through, they still judged him and treated him like he was a bad child. They also stopped talking to me and went out of their way to ignore me.

His teacher stopped wanting to interact with him and treated him differently as well. She treated him like he was a bad child and was misbehaving on purpose. It was a very hard time. Not only was I dealing with the stress and uncertainty of what was wrong with my child and the pain he was going through, I was also dealing with feelings of sadness, isolation, and shame, from being judged by the fellow moms and Caleb's teacher.

Thankfully, Caleb eventually got better. It was a hard time for us all to go through. It seemed like it was never going to end. Once it did, I never forgot how the other moms made me feel while dealing with that situation. I vowed to learn from it and to make sure I never made anyone feel that isolated and alone.

I shared this story because at some point we are all going to be facing difficult situations and challenges while raising our Special Needs Children. The last thing we will want to deal with, in addition to the challenges, is feeling ostracized and judged by those who are supposed to understand our lives the most.

ADVICE FOR NEWLY DIAGNOSED: "Always Celebrate Every Success"

It is important for you to get into the habit of looking for successes in your child's Journey to celebrate, no matter how big or small. Finding them and celebrating them fuels your hope and strength. Our children's successes often do not look like their Mainstream Peers. It's usually not one big accomplishment that occurs, but rather smaller ones they may meet as they are working towards the bigger goal.

A Mainstream Child learning to tie his shoes might achieve it after a few tries. Our children, however, will usually learn it in stages. You may have to celebrate the fact that they learned how to make the two rabbit ears, even though they haven't learned how to completely tie their shoes yet. A Mainstream Child might finally learn how to write their name after some time. You can celebrate the fact that your child was finally able to sit still for an uninterrupted 20-minute session to work on writing their

name. A Mainstream Child might be learning how to zip his coat and is finally able to do it. Our child might be working on the same goal and has finally learned how to connect the zipper to the anchor at the bottom. While their accomplishments are completely different, you can still celebrate the fact that your child is one step closer to meeting their overall goal.

These are just some examples. The point is you must look for those things to celebrate. Since learning doesn't come easy for most of our children, and those big breakthroughs are few and far between, you must find those little things to acknowledge to remind yourself that while your child has not mastered a particular skill, they are still making progress.

One of Caleb's IEP goals for years was for him to be able to button his clothes. I deemed this as an important skill to help move him towards greater independence in the future. After working on this goal for several years, he finally got it! We went out to dinner to Celebrate His Success! It made him feel good because he knew he had done something great, and it made us feel good because we felt like our child was learning and moving closer to being able to take care of himself.

ADVICE FOR NEWLY DIAGNOSED: "Don't Assume! ASK!

Earlier, I talked about how we Special Needs Families often live in a 'parallel universe.' I talked about how we exist in the unique world we've created for our children, while being a part of Mainstream Society. Because of this factor, many times we assume people should just know that we need certain things and accommodations for our children, and we become upset when they do not receive them.

Case in point: I recently read on social media where a mom was upset about the fact that the school didn't provide any accommodations for the Special Needs Students during her child's Pre-K Graduation evening event. She didn't like the fact that the Special Needs Graduates were not separated and had to sit amongst their Mainstream Peers. She

also didn't like the fact that they had to sit for an extended period during a prepared program. Many people responded that the school was negligent in doing their duty towards our children. They said her child and the other students should not have been treated that way, and something needed to be done at once to make sure accommodations were put into place to meet their needs going forward. I agreed 100%!

I later thought about this scenario, and about some of the previous situations I had been confronted with for Caleb. I realized in most cases, the school or any other coordinator of a large body event or facility, typically does not set out to purposefully do things that are going to be detrimental to our children. Most do not try to deliberately exclude or disregard them.

Sadly, I think most of the time when these things happen, the coordinators simply overlooked the fact that they needed to come up with an alternate plan focused solely on incorporating our Special Needs

Student's role in the event. Should this be something that automatically comes to their minds? Yes! Should this be something that our educational and community leaders think of when planning events? Yes! Does this always happen? Inevitably, No!

So, rather than running the risk of getting to an event and finding out at the last minute that special accommodations have not been made for Caleb and his peers, I choose to reach out beforehand to start that conversation. I choose to ask questions to find out what is going to be done to make sure Caleb and his peers can take part in the event and still feel comfortable and safe.

I will first find out who the coordinator is and will then set up a meeting or phone call with them. I will point out to them Caleb (and his peers) has Autism; he is not able to sit for long periods of time without eventually becoming disruptive; it is preferable that a designated space is assigned to them; ideally the space is not within the crowd of his Mainstream Peers; preferably, this space is at the end of a row, and near an exit if possible.

Finally, I ask if he and his peers can be recognized at the beginning of an event, so they won't have to sit and wait for an extended period. I also ask if it is okay for them to leave once their participation is over, should they choose. I am just sharing my expectations of what I think are reasonable accommodations for our children. Even if they choose not to take my specific recommendations, and they do things differently, I am still satisfied if the necessary accommodations are put into place. I always try to go into situations like this with an open mind and a willingness to negotiate. Ultimately, I expect, however, that a consensus will be reached on what is going to be done to make sure that our children's Special Needs are taken into consideration and their accommodations are met. They deserve this treatment just like their Mainstream Peers, who will also be attending the event.

On some occasions, I have even had to ask these questions of Caleb's earlier administrators who were planning Campus-wide events and have known him as their student for years. At first, I was offended by the fact that I even had to ask, and they didn't just automatically know that they needed to consider him and his peers' special needs when planning events. They all knew Caleb and he had Autism. How could they not know that he couldn't sit still and quietly during an event for an extended period? Didn't they know anything about my son after interacting with him during the school year?

It was easy to get caught up in those questions and have anger towards those who were doing the event planning and feel like they were purposefully disregarding the accommodations Caleb and his peers needed. After talking to the coordinators, however, I realized most of them were not purposefully ignoring the things Caleb and his classmates needed, but simply had not thought of it. As soon as I brought to their attention the things that were needed, they immediately complied! I could see from their reactions they simply hadn't considered those things because they didn't have anyone on the planning committee to represent our children's needs during the event.

Would I have liked them to have considered these things on their own? Absolutely, Yes! But just like we live in our own 'Universe,' we must remember most of the people we interact with in our daily lives live in the Mainstream 'Universe.' While our thoughts are always on our Special Needs Children and making sure their needs are met and they are included, an administrator's perspective is typically on their entire student body and not just our children when coordinating an event.

I am NOT letting them off the hook! Incorporating our Special Needs Children's accommodations into every event should happen automatically without anyone having to remind the coordinators. We all get to choose our battles, however. Rather than choosing to be angry and upset because they neglected to include our children's needs in their event planning, I choose to reach out to them beforehand to make sure that they do. Then, on the day of the event, I don't have to worry about showing up for something that is supposed to be a memorable occasion, only to learn that the accommodations haven't been made, and Caleb's special moment is marred because of it. Even with the strongest apologies afterwards, it is not going to change the fact that negative events occurred.

So, to best prevent this from happening, I encourage you to use my approach to reach out and make sure the coordinator has the information they need to best accommodate our children. If for some reason the event is put together on the spur of the moment or poorly planned, and I am not able to reach out to the coordinator beforehand, you can best believe the appropriate persons will be hearing from me the next day to discuss their lack of accommodations and considerations for our children.

I have been walking this Autism Journey for a while now. We only have so much energy to spend in our overwhelmingly demanding days. We already have so many battles to fight for our children. If we can prevent one from happening in the first place, why not take it? I have never asked for special and reasonable accommodations for Caleb and his peers and been told 'No.' In most cases, those in charge are more than happy to do whatever is necessary to make sure our children are comfortable and have what they need.

Just as it is our desire as parents for our Special Needs Children to have a great event and experience, typically, those coordinating the event have that same desire as well. I'm sure the last thing they want to see is Caleb running and jumping during the event and my having to run through a crowd of people after him. Hence, this often leads to their decision to accommodate my requests to have our children sitting at the end of the row near an exit, to permit them to be able to step outside the event quickly if needed; to allow our children to go first is possible, and to allow our children to leave the event after their participation. Each of these accommodations creates a win-win for everyone involved.

ADVICE FOR NEWLY DIAGNOSED: "Our Children Need Time"

I am a Ph. D. not an M.D. So, I am in no way an expert on our Special Needs Children's ability to learn, nor in the operation and mechanization of their brain. I can tell you, however, one of the most precious commodities our children have for learning, is Time. Time gives them the opportunity to practice a skill repeatedly, increasing the odds of them learning it.

A task that might take a Mainstream Child 2-3 months of practice, with 15-20 tries to learn, might take our Special Needs Child 1-2 years, if not longer, and 1000-2000 or more tries, just to obtain the same skill, if ever. And, once our child learns a new skill, there are no guarantees they will be able to continue doing it over the course of time. Regardless of our children's age, there are many things they 'should' know how to do in relation to their Mainstream Peers but based on the nature of their disability and cognitive level, they do not.

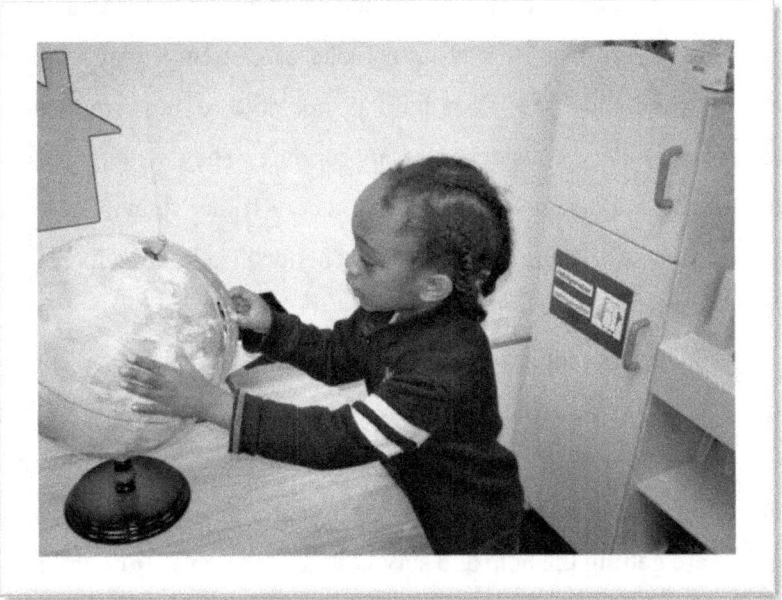

As a parent, it is not easy having to admit you can't teach your child basic skills such as how to brush their teeth, use a spoon, or bathe properly. You can show them and tell them 1000 times, but if you are not doing it in a way they can comprehend, then it is futile. As a member of Mainstream Society, we can only teach our children new skills in the same way they were taught to us. Unfortunately, in most cases these methods are ineffective when working with our Special Needs Children's learning styles.

Therefore, it is important for us Special Needs Parents to put our pride aside and acknowledge that we need help teaching our children, by getting them into some form of speech, occupational or physical therapy. Even though we are their parents and should be able to teach our children all they need to know, their learning needs are far beyond the skills that most of us parents possess. These therapists are trained to teach our children and communicate with them on a level they can better understand.

Please know, many times when you are out with your Special Needs Child, you may be met with looks of contempt and scorn from strangers when they see your child is not able to do something that Mainstream Society considers age appropriate. They will look at your child and assume because they are 'bigger' or 'older' they should know how to do certain things, or to behave better. Their judgement of our children is grossly inaccurate and unfair.

While these judgments can be extremely hurtful, we parents must hold our heads up high, put our shoulders back, and keep moving forward. Do not allow yourself to be weighed down with other people's opinions. Your child is going to need you to use all your energy and focus to make sure they are getting the help and services they need. Never doubt that you are the right person for the job of raising your child. There isn't anyone more perfect for this task than you.

ADVICE FOR NEWLY DIAGNOSED: "Life Will Be Different, But It Will Be Worth It."

To my readers who are just starting this Autism or Special Needs Journey, or are a little way into it, I am not trying to paint a rosy picture of what it is like to raise our Special Needs Children. I am forever an optimist. Therefore, I tend to always look for the good in every situation and to present things in a positive light. While that perspective may have spilled over into my writing, I want to be clear: **This Journey is Not Easy!** You will often find yourself having more challenging days than triumphant ones.

There will be many days you will feel like you are walking through quicksand, saying, and doing the same things over and over while making no progress. You will be so tired you can't even find the strength to go to bed. These things will become a part of your daily life and routine. They will become a part of the makeup of who you are. The person you were before you had your Special Needs Child will many times seem foreign and lost to you. You will wonder, where did the *Old* You go? And ask, how do you cope with the life of the *New* You?

Despite the many challenges you face, you will find a way to embrace all that life has for you at this stage, and you will find a way to make the best of it. It is my hope that by writing this book and advising and educating you on the things I have learned, it will make your Journey a bit easier as you walk down these long Autism Roads. The advice I shared came solely from my experiences of having to learn as I go. Hopefully, this information will help you to avoid some of those pitfalls I had; will help you know what questions to ask in different situations; and will give you a better idea of what to expect.

While there will be many dark days, you will have those occasional moments where your child will do something amazing; they have an unexpected breakthrough; or they may simply look you in the eyes for the first time and smile. These are the things that make all the difficult days worthwhile. These are the things that give you that last bit of fuel and spark you need to keep going and fighting for another day.

The times when I am having a hard day and Caleb takes my face in his hands and leans his forehead in towards me for a kiss; or he comes over and lays his cheek right against mine; or he raises his arm and says, *"I want Tickles Please!"* to connect with me, every challenge I am faced with in that moment fades away into the distance. And I am reminded once again of *Who* I am fighting for, *What* I am fighting for, and *Why* the toil and the pain are all worth it.

I know hearing your child's Diagnosis was hard. It took me over a year before I could even say the word *Autism* aloud, and another two years before I could talk openly about it and share Caleb's Journey with others. Even today, there are times when I still struggle with it.

It is not an easy job raising our Special Needs Children; but the rewards you get from the little things they do, and seeing the world through their eyes, makes your heart overflow with love and gratitude!

DR. RHONDA BROWN-CROWDER

CHAPTER EIGHT

"HE WILL SEND HELP!"

A t this point in the book, you must be wondering how you are going to survive this difficult Journey, to be there for your child, to give them the support that they need, and keep your sanity. I can tell you how… *GOD Will Send You Help!* That doesn't mean there won't still be difficult days, but HE will make sure the right people are strewn along the Roads you travel, to come into your life at the exact right time. They will give you the love, support, encouragement, knowledge, and strength you need, to keep from giving up and to continue your way.

While walking this Autism Journey, there have been so many wonderful people who have come into our lives. I call them "Caleb's Community." Without each of them giving us love, hope, strength, guidance, and support, neither Caleb nor I would be where we are today.

It's amazing how GOD orchestrated these people to come into Caleb's life to help him, and in the process, they ended up helping me as well. There are too many people to name that have been instrumental in our progress and success. These are Eight Key People who made a significant impact in our lives:

- ❖ **Jenetta Whitenight,** Caleb's first Pre-K /CARE Teacher for one-half year
- ❖ **Pamela Fowler,** Caleb's first Special Olympics Coach
- ❖ **Joe Taylor,** Founder of Miracle League Irving, Texas
- ❖ **Lanette Stewart,** Caleb's second Pre-K /CARE Teacher for one entire year
- ❖ **Chris O'Gorman,** Caleb's Special Olympics Peer Partner
- ❖ **Rebekah Bowe,** Fellow Special Needs Autism Mom, Advisor, Confidant, and Dear Friend
- ❖ **Alfi Thomas,** Licensed Clinical Counselor, Confidant, and Dear Friend

JENETTA WHITENIGHT, CALEB'S 1ST PRE-K, PPCD TEACHER

After Caleb was officially diagnosed with Autism and a Speech Impairment, a week before his fourth birthday, things moved quickly. I was still in a state of shock, trying to deal with the words *'Autism Spectrum Disorder,'* when we were scheduled for Caleb's first ARD (Admission Review Dismissal) Meeting.

Suddenly I found myself sitting in a board room surrounded by school administrators and professionals in various fields, discussing Caleb and setting learning goals for him. I had no idea what was going on. One of the ladies in the meeting said she was going to be Caleb's first teacher.

Her name was Mrs. Jenetta Whitenight. When we first heard her name, my husband and I joked about the fact that she was going to be Caleb's *'Night in Shining Armor.'* Little did we know this was going to be exactly the case.

I remember in the ARD meeting watching Mrs. Whitenight and listening to her. As they were talking about goals for Caleb, I kept thinking to myself, *"He can't do that." "How are they going to be able to get him to do that?"* And with every question I asked within myself, Mrs. Whitenight answered aloud, *"Yes! We can help him with that!"* I remember she was so confident in her responses that I too began to feel more confident in Caleb's ability to learn.

The first day I dropped Caleb off at Pre-K, he, and I both cried! Because Mrs. Whitenight seemed so certain that everything was going

to be okay, it made me feel a little bit better. Driving away from the school and leaving my child was the hardest thing I ever had to do!

Thankfully, by the end of the week, Caleb was all smiles!

Mrs. Whitenight and her paraprofessionals were wonderful! I was truly amazed at how quickly Caleb adjusted to being in school. He really surprised me! He acted as if he had been going all his life! A part of me was happy because it gave me peace of mind knowing he was enjoying being there and was okay; and another part of me, as a mom, felt a little sad because he seemed to be doing so well without me being there. I say this with humor of course, as I'm sure most moms (and dads) will completely understand my reaction.

I experienced so much fear and anxiety at the first stage of Caleb's Diagnosis. The gap between the things Caleb should be doing at his age in relation to his Mainstream Peers, seemed insurmountable. I was struggling to first accept the fact he had this Autism Diagnosis. I was then overwhelmed trying to better understand his unique needs; all while trying to remain hopeful that he could indeed learn and eventually close that gap. Mrs. Whitenight became my leaning post. I felt so lost! I found comfort and peace just from being in her presence.

Every morning when I took Caleb into her classroom, I watched Mrs. Whitenight or one of her paraprofessionals grab his hand and walk him over to hang up his coat and backpack. She then helped him take his folder out of his backpack and place it in a tray. She and her Paraprofessionals did all this hand-over-hand.

Caleb had no sense of awareness as to what was going on, nor any clue about what he was doing. As I watched him, I wondered so many times if he ever would. All the while, Mrs. Whitenight was consistent. Day-in and day-out she did the exact same thing. She and her wonderfully trained team of paraprofessionals were relentless in working with our children.

Since everything about Autism was new to me, I relied on Mrs. Whitenight's expertise to better educate myself. I spent a lot of time in her classroom, before and after Caleb's Pre-K half day morning session. I felt so much peace and comfort just from being in her presence, and in knowing she was someone who could help me make Caleb's life better.

Being in Mrs. Whitenight's presence gave me so much hope for Caleb and his ability to learn. On many occasions I would take Caleb to school early, before the sun rose, as Mrs. Whitenight was getting the classroom set up for the day. I did this just to ask questions and to glean from her knowledge. She never made me feel like I was a burden to her or in the way. She always made herself available to me.

There were so many days after Caleb's Diagnosis that I felt terrified! The thought of dealing with a lifetime of his Diagnosis was the scariest feeling I ever had. I felt so inadequate to walk this, Journey. I felt like I was going to fail Caleb. I remember so many times walking into Mrs.

Whitenight's classroom near tears, and after talking with her I left feeling stronger with renewed hope. Just hearing her tell me I was doing a good job with Caleb; I was a good mom, and everything was going to be okay, meant the world to me. Mrs. Whitenight expressed confidence in my ability to be a good mother and to be able to deal with the many things concerning Caleb. Her belief in me made me feel like I wouldn't fail.

On the days when I felt so overwhelmed from working full time, managing our household, pursuing my Doctorate, looking for outside services and therapies for Caleb, navigating through insurance companies, co-pays, and doctor's appointments, Mrs. Whitenight was there as a constant source of encouragement and support. I relied on her compassion and strength. For the days when I felt lost and like a complete failure because I had no idea what to do to help Caleb, Mrs. Whitenight was there. For the times when I felt hopeless and overwhelmed and wondered about Caleb's future and how he was going to survive in this world, Mrs. Whitenight was there.

Early one morning, when I was feeling my lowest, Mrs. Whitenight looked me in the eyes and told me one day I would be an Advocate for Special Needs Children and their Families. I laughed inside at the thought of that. Here I was feeling like I didn't have the strength to put one foot in front of the other; and she was speaking into my future saying one day I would Advocate for and help others on this same Journey.

In that moment, not only did I not want to be an Advocate, but I didn't even want to be in the situation of having to raise a child with Special Needs. A part of me just kept thinking that something 'magical' was going to happen and Caleb would just one day wake up and be a Mainstream Child again. This reaction was just my ill-equipped mind's way of trying to cope with the thought of raising a child on a life-long Autism Journey. I remember thinking, how can I be an Advocate for helping others when I don't even have a clue about what I am doing myself? And yet, here I am today, writing this book.

As my knowledge of Autism and Special Needs grew, so did my confidence in being able to deal with Caleb's Diagnosis. I realized, helping people, and sharing information is something that comes naturally for me. Advocating for and speaking on behalf of our Special Needs Community is my Passion. It is my Calling. As I look back on that time in my life, I am always so amazed that Mrs. Whitenight was able to see those qualities in me before I could see them in myself.

As time progressed and Caleb made it through his first half-year of Pre-K with Mrs. Whitenight, I was amazed at his progress! When he first started school, I was so concerned about the fact that he had no awareness of the things that were going on around him. Mrs. Whitenight and her paraprofessionals continued to do the same things repeatedly during his learning sessions in the classroom.

While it was a much later time when Caleb's awareness really started to increase, the hand-over-hand usage and consistency in routines in the classroom established a strong learning foundation for him. These things helped both Caleb and I to realize when placed in an environment that promoted routine and structure, he was capable of learning. The foundation that Mrs. Whitenight and her wonderful paraprofessionals laid for Caleb so many years ago is the same one that he continues to stand and build on today.

Mrs. Whitenight is one of the people I most admire in this world. She is completely oblivious as to how wonderful she is and what a lasting difference she makes. Her only focus is on making our children's lives better and preparing them for their future. From day one I have been in awe of her: her vast knowledge of teaching and working with children with Special Needs; her generous heart; her love and compassion; and her unending hope in believing that all children can learn regardless of their disabilities or limitations.

When I think of GOD sending each of us to this earth with a specific assignment and purpose to carry out and to make a difference, Mrs. Whitenight comes to mind. Everything she touches and everything she does becomes better than it was before.

Today, Mrs. Whitenight remains as my mentor, my confidant, my greatest resource, and one of my dearest friends. As Caleb continues to progress throughout his lifetime, I will always attribute his continued

growth, learning, and success to Mrs. Whitenight, because she was the one who laid the strong foundation at the beginning of his educational Journey.

GOD Almighty knew I needed Mrs. Whitenight in my life to start Caleb and I down the right Roads of this challenging Autism Journey. Not only was she in my life then, but she remains in my life today. It is such a wonderful feeling to be able to share all of mine and Caleb's growth and accomplishments throughout the years with her. I always tell her all the great things happening in mine and Caleb's lives today, started with HER! We are the fruit of her labor. We are forever grateful for the time, energy, and heartfelt effort she poured into our lives. We will forever be a *"Whitenight Kid and Whitenight Mom!"*

PAMELA FOWLER, SPECIAL OLYMPICS COORDINATOR & ADAPTIVE PE COACH

I first met Coach Pam when Caleb was six years old. Because he was not old enough yet to compete in Special Olympics, the School District had an Annual Event called "YAP" (Young Athletes Program) for the underage athletes to come together and have a fun day of activities. This event was held for one day and it included a series of mock games

and activities mimicking many of the various Special Olympics Sports the athletes would be able to take part in. The first time Caleb attended this event was in Mrs. Whitenight's Pre-K class. It was the first time I had ever seen him playing and interacting with other children. I was fascinated watching his extreme joy and excitement!

I was also excited because we parents were able to join our children at

the event. It was held shortly after Caleb's Autism Diagnosis, and it was both mine and Caleb's first introduction to being around other Special Needs Children and their Families.

Coach Pam was the coordinator of this event. She ran it like a well-oiled machine! As I watched this woman moving to-and-fro across this large building at 100 mph, I was fascinated with her obvious passion for what she did and her ability to coordinate such a huge event. Special Needs Students from all over the district were there. I introduced myself

to her before the event ended. I told Coach Pam how excited I was for Caleb to be able to participate in Special Olympics. She informed me he had to be at least eight years old to compete. Our life-long bond and friendship began to form in that moment.

For two additional years, Coach Pam and I would see each other at the YAP Event. Caleb had not yet turned eight during that second year. We shared our excitement about him finally being able to start taking part in Special Olympics in the coming fall, after his birthday. Each time he took part in the YAP event, Caleb had the time of his life! It was so much fun watching him smiling and enjoying playing and interacting with those around him!

When Caleb was finally old enough to join Special Olympics, I was so excited he could participate in sports. There are so many sports opportunities for Mainstream Children, but very few for those in our Special Needs Community. Since this was a new venture, I had no idea what to expect.

Even though Coach Pam had worked with Special Needs Athletes for over 20 years, I didn't know if working with my rambunctious little Caleb was going to prove to be too much of a challenge. From the first practice on, I saw the great level of skill, expertise, love, patience, and accountability Coach Pam utilized when working with Caleb and the other athletes, and in setting expectations for their behavior and performance.

Caleb's very first after-school-practice with Coach Pam was for basketball. I was still in the mindset that nothing others tried to teach

our Special Needs Children had to be in a Mainstream learning mode. I had no idea about all the adaptive sports options available to our children; so, based on that perspective, I couldn't see any way Caleb would be able to comprehend playing basketball in the traditional sense. I was very curious to see how Coach Pam was going to teach him.

Watching Coach Pam working with Caleb was magical. It gave me such a great sense of pride. From the point of Caleb's Autism Diagnosis and the beginning of his Journey, I had never experienced this magnitude of feelings before. He was running with her, warming up with her, stretching with her, and doing all the things she asked him to do even though he had never done any of those things before.

Caleb was smiling, excited, and totally engaged. He also listened to her and was calm and in control of himself. As I saw their interactions, I suddenly started seeing My Caleb in a totally different light. The doors of my mind swung wide open, and I began to realize there were tons of new possibilities for the things he could do.

Coach Pam informed me she didn't think Caleb was ready to play the basketball team sport, but she felt he would do great competing in basketball skills. Watching Caleb dribble a ball for the first time, do wall passes, and shoot the ball through hanging hoola hoops made me ask myself, *"Who is this Child?!"* I had no idea he could do any of those things because we never tried them. I feel sad and deeply ashamed to say, at that time I just assumed he couldn't do them.

For every new sport Coach Pam recommended Caleb try, he excelled in them. When she said confidently, he would be able to run the 50-yard-dash on his own, I couldn't even imagine it. But after months of practice and her working with Caleb, he was ready to compete in his first track meet. Coach Pam stood with him at the start line and told him to run to me at the finish line. I didn't know what to expect! I just hoped he

would at least stay on the track!! When he crossed the finish line, and leaped into my arms, I was over the moon with excitement and joy! You can't even begin to imagine how proud I was of him when he did it! He ran an entire 50-yard dash all by himself! I was beaming!

The most amazing takeaway from this experience was, anytime Coach Pam asked Caleb to do something he had never done before, he never pulled back from the unknown nor refused to try new things. He rather stepped up and just did them with ease. Suddenly, I realized I had a natural athlete on my hands. Not only was I proud of Caleb as a mother; but seeing the look of joy and excitement on his face after realizing he had done something new, was spectacular and priceless!

The joy and excitement I felt after watching Coach Pam working with Caleb in after school practice, and then seeing him demonstrate those skills during competitions, brought tears to my eyes. Caleb performed as

if he had done them a thousand times. Coach Pam was there with him, every step of the way. Her presence and belief in him gave him the confidence he needed to succeed.

Coach Pam is a humble, yet mighty leader. Over the course of a 30-year career, she worked with thousands of Special Needs Athletes at all ages and stages of abilities. She inspired the athletes to do more and to be more. Everything she did with Caleb and his fellow athletes was impactful and lasting. She didn't lower her standards and expectations because of their disabilities, but rather raised them to a level she knew each athlete could meet.

Coach Pam not only went above and beyond to build relationships with the athletes, but with our Special Needs Parents and Families as well. She understood the importance of parental involvement in the lives of our children and its contributions to their success. Caleb experienced tremendous growth, calmness, focus, self-regulation, and excitement under her leadership. I learned so much from her as well!

One day as Caleb and I were leaving track practice, I said goodbye to Coach Pam. Her response was, *"Thank You for allowing me to coach your son."* Her use of the word, *"allow,"* touched me deeply. In a world where we Special Needs Parents are doing all we can to make sure our children feel loved and accepted by the Mainstream World, her use of the word *"allow"* said it all.

It spoke to her character, her life's work, focus, dedication, and commitment to what she does. It reflected her heart to help others and to let them know they matter. Just the thought of her using that word brought tears to my eyes then, and it brings tears to my eyes now.

As a Parent of a child with Special Needs, it is rare to find someone who cares about Caleb's identity, his future, well-being, and self-esteem as much as I do. Coach Pam showed that she did also. She not only challenged our children, but she made them feel loved and valued. She showed them that they mattered.

I was so honored to write a nomination for Coach Pam for the

National "Life Changer of the Year" Award. Out of thousands of submissions from across the country, she was one of the few recipients who was chosen to receive the award. I don't know who was prouder in the moment of her recognition: me, for being able to submit a nomination for such an amazing and deserving person; or her, for being the recipient. It was such a joyous occasion that I will always treasure, and we will always share!

GOD brought Coach Pam into my life to show me all the wonderful things Caleb could do that I didn't even realize. She expressed so much confidence and assurance in Caleb's ability to excel in new things, I couldn't help but believe it as well. The greatest gift she gave me was a new perspective and way of seeing My Caleb. When she showed me through Special Olympics Sports that Caleb was capable of learning new things and enjoying them, she gave our lives a whole new meaning.

Now, when I look at Caleb and an idea comes to mind about something new, I want him to try, I no longer dismiss it or shut it down. I now say, *"Let's Try It!"* Each time, Caleb has risen to the occasion! He now knows how to roller skate; he loves to rock climb; he flew with me in a small engine plane; he did indoor skydiving with me, he enjoys baking in the kitchen, creating wonderful paintings, and So Much More! Yes, there are some things he prefers to do more than others, but had we not tried, we would have never known.

Coach Pam's many years of hard work and dedication in working with our children, and really getting to know them, allowed her to connect with Caleb on his level. She brought out hidden treasures in him that I, his mother, never knew existed. Not only did GOD send Coach Pam into Caleb's life, but into mine as well. She was, and has remained, a beautiful friend, a confidant, a great source of strength, and someone who willingly shares her knowledge to help make life better for all Special Needs Children and Families. It was because of Coach Pam I decided to become a Certified Special Olympics Coach not just to work with My Caleb, but with other Special Needs Athletes as well. There is nothing more fulfilling than helping them compete and watching them excel!

There are few people in my life that I feel I can completely let my guard down with and fully be myself. Coach Pam is one of them. I am always the person others turn to when they need encouragement, support,

and their strength renewed. I willingly give of myself to them without hesitation. I am the leaning post they can count on when they need it the most. It comes naturally for me to be that person for others because I am a giver and a nurturer. It is rare, however, for me to find someone that I can go to when I need those same things in return.

Coach Pam has helped me through many difficult days. She has given me a shoulder to cry on; she has prayed with me; she has helped me to refocus and see things more clearly; she has helped to calm me down and reason things out before I acted on impulse.

When she tells me I can call her anytime day or night, she means it. There has never been a time when I needed her, that she was not there, even while dealing with her own life challenges. I trust her implicitly. I can be myself with her, and I can share my heart without fear or reservation. I love her dearly and admire her so much. I draw strength just from being in her presence.

Coach Pam is one of the most remarkable people I have ever met. She is someone whose footsteps can never be filled and whose impact can never be duplicated. I am so blessed to have her in my life and to call her my friend. I love how since her retirement she still shares in Caleb's successes and has such a great sense of pride in watching him grow and accomplish new things. I attribute so much of his growth and maturity to his time spent with her.

We are so deeply grateful GOD ordained our life's paths to cross with Coach Pam. She is one of HIS chosen vessels; someone who is deeply caring and giving; and such a wonderful human being.

JOE TAYLOR, MIRACLE LEAGUE BASEBALL FOUNDER, IRVING, TX. MOTIVATOR, DEAR FRIEND

Like most parents, I wanted Caleb to play sports. I wanted to see him in his uniform looking cute and taking lots of pictures. As Caleb got older and I considered what sports he might play, it was a depressing moment. I had to be realistic with myself and acknowledge he would not be able to keep up with his Mainstream Peers, while playing on a traditional team. I also had to consider the fact that he might be bullied or picked on as well.

Thankfully, around that time our local YMCA created a program they co-sponsored with another YMCA in a neighboring city. They agreed to cover the cost for our children with Special Needs to play baseball. It would be in the Miracle League Program. I was So excited! Even though I knew Caleb would likely not understand the dynamics of the game in the beginning, I was just happy for him to have a safe place to play where he could have fun and feel accepted and celebrated.

At the start of Caleb's second season on the team, one of the volunteer coaches pulled me aside and told me about "Mr. Joe." She said he was the one who brought the Miracle League Program to Irving, and he was the one our Miracle League Baseball Field was named after. She then pointed him out to me as he was sitting near the bleachers. I felt so bad because I realized I had been going to the games for over a year and had seen him, but I had no idea who he was. Before I left the game that day, I went up to him and introduced myself and thanked him for bringing such a wonderful program in which our children could take part.

For the next two years, after I became the Coach of Caleb's team, I had the pleasure and honor of really getting to know Mr. Joe on a personal level. Once I got to know him and his character, I realized it was not strange after all, that I didn't know the important role he played in impacting my son's life. Because Mr. Joe was not someone who would ever brag about how instrumental he was in making a difference in Caleb's life and in the lives of thousands of other Special Needs Children.

Mr. Joe was someone whose list of accolades and accomplishments was immeasurable. While he achieved so many wonderful things in life and earned every right to boast and think highly of himself, he did not. He did absolutely nothing to draw any attention to himself. He was one of the most humble, unassuming, and down-to-earth people I had ever known.

About a year before Mr. Joe passed away, we discussed my trying to get a Miracle League Field built in our City of Grand Prairie. When he first told me he thought I could make it happen. I smiled and said, *'Thank you,'* but I really didn't believe it in my heart. I thought that task was too great for me. When we talked again at the next game he put his arm

around my shoulder, looked me in the eyes, and told me again, he believed I was the one to bring the Miracle League Field to our city.

I can't fully put it into words, but something inside my spirit connected with what he was saying. I felt in my heart of hearts that he was speaking prophetically into my life, and this was a Mission that GOD had called me to do. I felt an overwhelming sense of excitement at the possibility of bringing it to pass.

A short time later, as Mr. Joe lay on his death bed and I sat at his side holding his hand, I whispered in his ear, *"Thank You, Mr. Joe, for believing in me." "Thank You for the gift you have given to Caleb and thousands of other children with Special Needs. I pledge to you that I will do all that is within my power, for as long as I live, to bring your dream to pass for getting a Miracle League Baseball Park built in our city."*

After I spoke those words to Mr. Joe, he squeezed my hand. While I left the hospital feeling so incredibly sad at the thought of him leaving this world, I also felt so eternally grateful that I had the opportunity to tell him how much he meant to me, and how knowing him changed my life forever. I felt so humbled and blessed that GOD allowed me to know and befriend such a great man.

While we didn't get a Miracle League Field built in our city, my meeting with then Parks Director Rick Herold to make my request, led me to an even greater project. He said, *"I can't promise you we will build a Miracle League Field, but you came by at the right time! We are about to build an All Access / All Abilities Park here in our city, unlike anything else in the Country, and we could use your help! It's going to be Epic!"*

Based on that meeting and invitation, I became a part of the Advisory Committee for the PlayGrand Adventures Park Project. My participation has allowed me to provide crucial parental input for this Park that was constructed specifically to accommodate our Special Needs Children and Adult's Abilities including, assisting with the equipment selected, the colors, location and placement of the items, sensory considerations, and much more. I have been a part of this project from its inception and planning to its groundbreaking, and now to its continued multi- phase buildout, to date.

The involvement I've had in this project has far exceeded anything I could have ever accomplished with a local Miracle League Project. The impact it's had on the lives of Special Needs Children, their families, and the community, is immeasurable. Families travel from surrounding cities and outside areas to visit this unique Park. It serves as a model and reminder to other cities throughout the country of the importance for them to also create safe places for their Special Needs Population to play.

The most exciting part of this project is, not only does it provide a space where a mobility-challenged dad can have a play experience with his child; a visually impaired person can enjoy reading Braille plaques while at play; a child in a wheelchair can enjoy being on a swing or merry-go-round designed especially for them, or a mother and daughter can enjoy a face-to-face swing experience. It also provides the joy of a side-by-side play experience where a Special Needs Child and a Mainstream Child can play together. It removes the barriers; and all you hear are the harmonious noises of children's laughter as it fills the air; and the only thing you see are the happy smiles on everyone's faces, parents, and children alike.

I was so grateful Mr. Joe lived to attend the meetings outlining the vision of the PlayGrand Park, and the unique purpose it would serve in our Special Needs Community. He was so incredibly excited and proud to know I was involved in the project! He also agreed it would far exceed bringing a Miracle League Field to our city!

Because of Mr. Joe, Caleb has been able to discover new talents he never knew he had. He has a fun, safe place to play on a team where he feels loved, valued, and accepted. Mr. Joe was willing to put all his successes, accomplishments, and accolades aside, to simply devote his time here to making life better for others. He was truly a Man of Honor.

MRS. LANETTE STEWART, CALEB'S 2ND PRE-K, PPCD TEACHER

After Caleb was Diagnosed with Autism, he spent the remaining school year in Mrs. Whitenight's Pre-K class. She was making amazing progress with him, and I was feeling more secure in my parenting role. I really liked her and was gleaning from all her knowledge and experience.

After Caleb completed Mrs. Whitenight's class, I was told during the summer break they were restructuring the PPCD program at his school, and it might no longer fully meet his needs. I was given the choice to let him remain at his current school with Mrs. Whitenight for one more year, or to elect to move him to another school, where he would eventually be going to kindergarten.

I felt like the rug had been pulled out from under me! I was still trying to come to terms with Caleb's Autism Diagnosis. I felt a certain level of comfort with his current teachers, the campus, and his routine; and now, I was faced with having to make a change within a few short months. Unfortunately, at that time, I hadn't learned something valuable that I now know: THINGS ARE EVER-CHANGING WITH OUR SPECIAL NEEDS CHILDREN! Therapists, teachers, administrators, and staff members all come and go for a variety of reasons.

If I had my way, the specialists and teachers in Caleb's life would never change; but that is not the way the world works. I had no idea what to do, as I had never been in that situation before. After talking with Mrs. Whitenight to get her advice, based on her glowing recommendation of Caleb's new teacher, I decided to go ahead and move him to the new campus. He was placed in Mrs. Lanette Stewart's class.

Mrs. Stewart was one of the kindest people I have ever known. I felt connected to her at once when I learned she had a Special Needs Son of her own, whom she was still caring for into adulthood. I knew this dynamic would cause her to immediately understand things about our lives that others would not. She was the most caring and compassionate person, not only with Caleb, but with me as a parent as well. Caleb absolutely loved being in her class! She had a unique way of teaching using arts, crafts, and various objects that allowed the students to explore hands on with different sensory items and textures. It was a perfect accompaniment for Caleb's learning style.

Not only was Mrs. Stewart great for Caleb, but she was great for me as well. Since this Autism Journey was still so new to me, I needed a lot of handholding, hugs, and reassurance. I had a lot of questions as well. She never once made me feel like I was a bother to her, nor did I inconvenience her in any way. Caleb absolutely loved her as well. When he was in her presence, it was so obvious he not only loved her, but he felt comforted and safe with her. Seeing his reaction to her gave me great comfort as well.

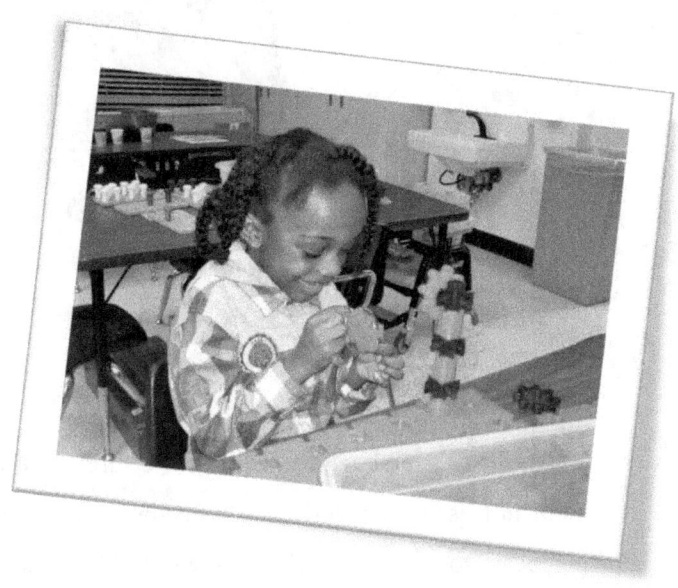

After Caleb left Mrs. Stewart's Pre-K class, and went to kindergarten and his new campus, we remained in touch. She continued to make herself available when I needed her, and she helped me to navigate through the vast paperwork and processes of getting Caleb the outside services he needed.

When our family was looking for a church home where we could go and worship freely, while not having to worry about Caleb being disruptive in the service (because it's hard for him to sit still and remain quiet for long periods of time), she welcomed us to her church. Her husband JD was the Pastor. He was well known and respected as a lifelong resident of our city. They welcomed us with open arms!

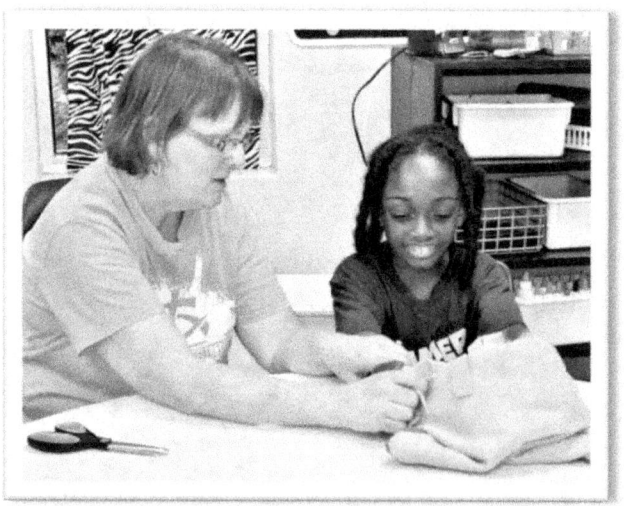

Mrs. Stewart took Caleb back to Children's Church and would sit with him and help him as he did activities with the other Mainstream Children. It brings tears to my eyes to think about all the times I went to church needing to have time alone with GOD and have my Spirit renewed, and her taking Caleb to Children's Church allowed me to do so.

There is no way I would have gotten anything out of the service if Caleb was there with me because I would have constantly been trying to keep him quiet and making sure he wasn't being disruptive. Mrs. Stewart and Pastor JD gave me the "Gift" of having time along with GOD.

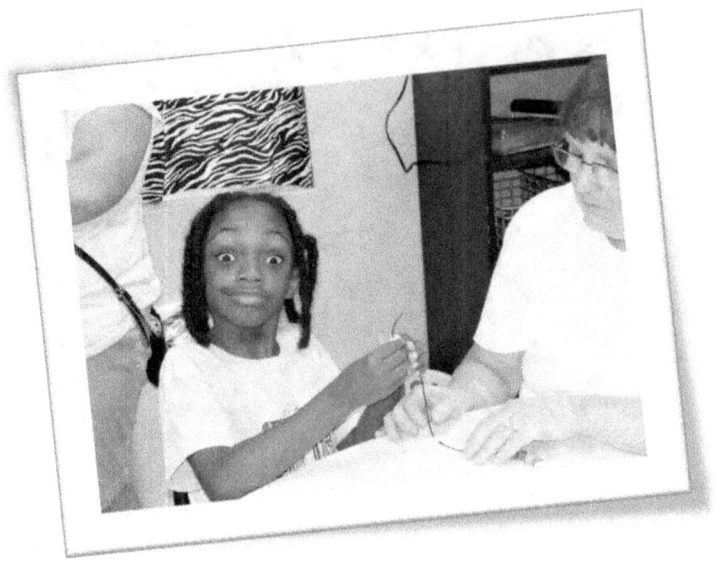

During those times, all I could do was exhale and Thank GOD for allowing me to have that much needed escape. To this day, Mrs. Stewart is someone that I deeply admire and respect. I am so happy that GOD saw fit to write it in our Life's Plan for our paths to cross during this Autism Journey. We are so blessed to know her and to call her our friend for life, and to have precious memories of time spent with her late husband Pastor JD as well.

UPDATE: My heart is deeply saddened to share, as I was finishing the final edits of this book, Mrs. Stewart passed away unexpectedly. While she had not yet read all the wonderful things, I had to say about her; I had told her them many times before. She knew I was featuring her in my book, and how much Caleb and I both loved her.

I feel even more honored now to share with the world what a wonderful person she was, and the significant difference she made in our lives. She will be profoundly missed and forever remembered.

CHRIS O'GORMAN, CALEB'S SPECIAL OLYMPICS PEER PARTNER OF 4 YEARS

There have been a host of things said about Millennials / Generation Y. Concerns have been expressed about their ability to look beyond themselves and to care about the needs of others. Many have shared some trepidation at the thought of what our world will be like in 20 years once they are in decision making position. When I met Millennial Chris O'Gorman, Caleb's Special Olympics Peer Partner of four years, I knew with other Millennials like him, our world was going to be a much better, more enriched place; and they would leave it better off than they found it.

Chris was a high school student who committed to being a Special Olympics Peer Partner for our athletes. He completely dedicated himself to working with Caleb to help him compete in Special Olympics bowling, basketball, and track and field.

While Chris's peers were out doing typical teenager things, he was out on the track field at practice, helping Caleb to focus on staying in his lane while running. While his peers were making sure they had the

latest clothes and other fads, Chris was in the gym in shorts and a t-shirt working with Caleb teaching him how to shoot through hoola hoops. While his peers were hanging out and spending time together, Chris was going to Special Olympics events to help Caleb compete in bowling and spent time walking with him to help keep him calm when he became overwhelmed. While his peers were going to the latest parties and social events, Chris was meeting with Caleb and I to practice dance routines so we could all compete in the Special Education Talent Shows. There are so many other examples I could give about this remarkable young man!

Never have I met someone who was so young with such a heart to care for and show compassion and patience for our Special Needs Children. Never have I met someone so young who was so dedicated to not only helping our children, but to continually educating himself on learning ways to be more effective in working with them. Never have I met someone so young whose life's path, in working with the Special Needs Community, was so crystal clear.

Caleb and I have been so blessed to have been a part of the start of Chris's incredible life's Journey. Even after he graduated from high school, Chris continued to remain in Caleb's life. He attended baseball games with us; he went to Special Events Concerts with us; he worked at Caleb's weeklong overnight camp as a counselor; and he supported Caleb in his Miracle League Baseball and Special Olympics endeavors. It was only after he moved away to college that we stopped seeing Chris on a regular basis. When Caleb got to see him again, during the holidays after an extended period, the reunion between them was beautiful and heart-warming.

I feel some people are called to a higher purpose in life, to do great things that are life-changing for others. I believe Chris is one of those people. The impact he has had on Caleb's life, and even in mine as a parent, is immeasurable. Words cannot adequately express how grateful I feel. I know that Chris has a full and accomplished life ahead of him. I look forward to Caleb and I remaining a part of it and seeing the Great Things GOD has in store for him!

REBEKAH BOWE, FELLOW AUTISM MOM, SPECIAL NEEDS ADVOCATE, MENTOR, DEAR FRIEND

I first met Rebekah at a Special Education PTA Meeting a few months after Caleb was Diagnosed with Autism. At that time, I had no idea where to start in learning things to help him. A couple of years went by before mine and Rebekah's paths crossed again. I had learned a little more about Autism, but there were still vast amounts of information I yet needed to know.

Rebekah told me My Caleb reminded her of her son David when he was younger. She said they were of the same build, both had high energies, loved to run and jump, and knew how to turn on the charm to get out of doing things when they needed to. She said because she saw her son David in my son Caleb, she felt drawn to us and wanted to help us as we walked the Autism Paths she and David had already completed.

There are so many sides to this Autism Journey. You could be getting along just fine, thinking that you know and have done everything that is needed at that stage in your child's life, only to learn that there are many other things you didn't know about, nor even knew to ask. Rebekah is THE most knowledgeable and diligent person I know when it comes to Autism Services, Federal Laws and Rights for our Special Needs Children, Educational Laws and Statutes, Preparing for Life 'Beyond the Bell,' and so much more. I have known her now for years, and every time I talk to her, I still walk away with new knowledge and ways I can better help Caleb get the services and help that he needs.

I am a person who often thinks and processes things with my heart, while Rebekah is someone who thinks and processes things with her head. I know GOD sent her into mine and Caleb's lives not only to help us get him all the services he's entitled to, but to make sure I have a more balanced approach when making decisions concerning him. I really appreciate the fact that Rebekah is straight-forward and tells me what she thinks. She apologizes first, but I always tell her I appreciate the fact that she is looking out for me and wants to make sure I am looking at things from the right perspective for Caleb.

Because of Rebekah, Caleb has attended an expensive, weeklong, overnight summer camp for years; he received grant monies for years for speech, occupational, and music therapy. He was supplied a personal assistant, that I wasn't even aware he qualified for, to help lighten my load; he attended special needs performances at our prestigious symphony; he received a new iPad and expensive communication software; he received services from one of the best therapy facilities, and so much more!

Rebekah has been a constant source of strength for me as well. Because her son David is older than Caleb, I can lean on her when the Autism Journey gets hard and I'm wondering how I'm going to make it. She encourages me along the way. She also caused me to look at Caleb's learning in a different way. As he got older, she helped me to realize that while academic learning is important, at some point I had to shift my way of thinking and start focusing on developing Caleb's functional skills.

She helped me to realize that this is the only way Caleb would truly have a chance at living an independent life. She also helped me to understand learning occurs everywhere, whether inside or outside the classroom. And she helped me to realize the importance of remaining flexible and open to teaching the way our children learn, and not necessarily to the way our Mainstream Institutions require. Rebekah helped me to realize learning for our children should not be cookie-cutter and by-the-book but should be as individualized as they are. As she likes to say when it comes to her son David's learning, *"We Do Real Life!"*

Rebekah helped me to see the importance of making sure Caleb is learning things that are going to aid him in life. It is not saying learning other educational skills are not important; but as they get older, we must also prioritize the things that are the most conducive in helping our children to have a better chance at living a more independent life.

As I mentioned previously, as Caleb got older, I had to come to the realization that his need to learn functional life skills superseded my desire for him to learn the things Mainstream Education considered most important. What good would it do if Caleb could read a full paragraph on his own, but couldn't dress or feed himself? While utilizing that Mainstream Educational skill would be great, it would not serve him in the way he needed the most: assisting him in living a more independent life by being better able to take care of himself.

Embracing this new-found philosophy has been life-changing for me in the way that I teach Caleb and in my expectations of him. When outside, I now look for ways to teach him through nature. Now, when doing any activity, I look for ways to incorporate counting, turn-taking, active listening, cleaning up, sorting items, and so much more. I found Rebekah's way of thinking opened my mind to new and endless possibilities!

I first thought I would teach Caleb how to use a microwave, do laundry, and other functional things when he was older. I realized; however, I could start working on those things with him now and give him that much more time to practice the new skills. I now understand learning doesn't have to be on a set schedule or timetable, and it's okay if our children don't learn like their Mainstream Peers. At the end of the day, we parents must remember our number one priority is to help our children become as independent as possible.

Having my dear friend Rebekah in my life caused me to open my mind to new things; to not always follow the norm; and to always remember that I am the one GOD sent to care for Caleb. I am the one who gets to decide what is best for him and how to structure his life in a way I think is going to be the most rewarding for him without offering any apologies or explanations.

Rebekah not only helped me to understand these things at the beginning of Caleb's Autism Journey, but she is still a blessing in our lives today. For each new stage we enter, Rebekah continues to reach back and share her knowledge of the things she and David have encountered and learned, to make things easier for us and others.

I marveled at the fact that when she couldn't find a program that fully embraced David's Special Needs and gave him something meaningful to do as an adult, Rebekah created one! He now has his own business where he creates and paints original, one-of-a-kind arts and crafts pieces, for those who are looking to purchase a priceless gift, while supporting an Autistic Entrepreneur. These items can be found through #victoriousvibrantbowe and #teambowe.

Rebekah is not only a tremendous blessing to me but to so many others as well. I treasure her friendship! I deeply admire and respect her as well. She gives me strength and courage, and she helps me feel empowered. When I am overwhelmed, she allows me to be weak and lets me know that everything is going to be okay. Her actions show me she not only cares about her son and family, but also about me, My Caleb, and our family as well.

ALFI THOMAS, LICENSED CLINICAL SOCIAL WORKER, CONFIDANT, AND DEAR FRIEND

It's so interesting how people can walk into your life, and immediately you know they were always meant to be there. You go through the formalities of getting to know each other, but deep inside

you feel like you've already met long ago. You find there is a place in your heart that has been unfulfilled, and then suddenly you realize, this person is the perfect fit. This description is what my dear friend Alfi's friendship means to me.

I can't fully explain what it is about Alfi that made us become instant friends, and why it is that I trust her with all that I am; but she is all those things to me and more. I met her when she came to a nonprofit agency where I worked to do her Internship as a Social Worker. At that time, she was single, with no children, and I was married with a newly Diagnosed Special Needs Son. It would seem as if we had nothing in common, but for some reason we bonded. But from the moment we met, our friendship remained through her getting married and eventually becoming a mother herself. Nothing about our relationship changed. It just became more enriched.

The depth of our friendship increased because the heart Alfi has and the qualities she possesses never changed. For reasons unbeknownst to me, I feel complete love, peace, and acceptance in her presence. I can experience each of those feelings separately, in a multitude of places with a variety of people, but rarely all of them with one person.

Very few people get to see me in my moments of fatigue, hopelessness, weakness, and despair. Usually when I am feeling that way, I don't remain in that state for long. When it is the case that those feelings linger, and I start wondering if I am ever going to be able to pull myself up out of a dark pit, I go through the long list of 'friends' in my mind wondering who I can call. It's hard for me to let others see me mentally bloody and bruised, feeling lost and alone.

Many people say they will be there for you, but most do not really want to see us in a weakened and frail state. It's okay, however, because they really don't know how to handle us in those moments. It's because that is not the person, they are accustomed to dealing with; they don't know the right things to say in those moments; and they don't know what the appropriate things are to do.

When I am having one of those dreadful moments, I call Alfi. I tell her I am in desperate need of a break. She will do whatever is necessary to rearrange her schedule to make time for me. As soon as I see her face and her smile, I immediately feel better. I start to feel the weight of the world lifting off my shoulders.

I think one of the things I appreciate so much from being in Alfi's presence is the feeling of nonjudgement. No matter what I tell her; no matter how I am feeling; no matter what my struggles are, she just listens. Because of this, I can talk to her about anything. And simply having that outlet is the one thing I need the most. Alfi provides a safe space for me to share the things that are killing me on the inside, wearing me down, and hurting my heart. I always leave her presence feeling better and stronger.

I know she is a confidant and someone that I can fully trust, and I never have to worry about her sharing my information with others or later using my words against me. Alfi always tells me I am a Super Woman. If I were to refer to that analogy, I would say she allows me to be Clark Kent, and to just be me when I need to just let my guard down and get that much needed break.

The best part is, she lets me know she loves and admires me as much for the person I am, Rhonda Rochelle, as she does for me as a Mother, Wife, Ph.D., Special Needs Advocate, Professional, and so much more.

We don't get to see each other every day, but every time we come together again, it feels as if no time has passed. I could spend time with Alfi and talk to her for hours. I am so incredibly blessed that GOD has brought such a rare and amazing person into my life. I love the fact that we both share the same heart and we both care so much about

helping others. I will always cherish the time I get to spend with Alfi. She is my dearest friend for life.

CHAPTER NINE
"CROSSES TO BEAR"

My Pastor talked about how the Bible tells us that in this life we will all have 'crosses' to bear. He said the things that make you cry and break your heart the most are your 'crosses' to bear in this life. They are the biggest challenges that we face.

When I consider the ironies of life and how I was able to obtain the highest degree this world can offer, a Ph.D., and yet I have a son who struggles with learning every day, my heart breaks. When I consider how I can easily get up in front of people to speak and sing, and I am able to use my voice to encourage and inspire; and, yet, I have a son who struggles to put two words together to communicate his most basic needs, my heart breaks. All these many contradictions I face daily make me cry a multitude of tears.

I am not saying our Special Needs Children are our "crosses" to bear. I would never think or say that! It is the things our children must go through each day; the many obstacles they struggle to overcome; the feelings of being ostracized by their peers and society; and their continued quest to feel loved, valued, and accepted in this world, these are the weight of the crosses we Special Needs Parents must bear. We bear them because we parents must watch our children face the giants of rejection and isolation, every day. And we often feel powerless because we can't turn our children's situations around and make the world love and see them the way that we do.

It makes me feel sad that Caleb and all the other Special Needs Children must go through such difficult challenges every day. They are just innocent human beings trying to navigate through this event called life. They are often overlooked, ridiculed, discarded, and not accepted because of a Diagnosis they had no control over.

How can a child be judged for dealing with something over which they have no control? How can any child be made to feel as if their life and existence here on this earth does not matter? GOD said they matter. HE sent them here just the way they are. Who gave those in society the right to condemn our children and to go against the Word of All Mighty GOD?!

Our children must tap into a level of bravery that most children can't comprehend, just to move around in a society that was not designed for them. My heart applauds all of us Special Needs Parents and Families who give up so much of our own lives, goals, and dreams to do all we can to make a better life and environment for our children to dwell in. It makes me incredibly sad to see how we are judged and shunned and criticized for our parenting skills, when we are simply doing the very best, we can to create a better quality of life for our child.

I was hesitant at the beginning of Caleb's Autism Diagnosis to tell others about it because I didn't want them to judge him and think less of him as a person. It makes me sad because so many people look at Caleb and have already decided that at his tender young age, his future is already nil. They have decided he will not amount to anything. They have decided he is less of a human, and his life does not matter as much as his Mainstream Peers.

They are ashamed of him. They think all my efforts to care for him, to teach him, and to help him, are futile. They think my time could be better spent doing other things, like pursuing my career and climbing the Corporate Ladder. They would rather me put Caleb on the back burner and focus solely on myself. What they don't understand is, how could I put my life and dreams before caring for My Caleb? How could I have or enjoy any personal success when I know my child's needs aren't being met? How could any human being turn their back on own their child and stop fighting for them to have the chance of a better life? For me, making sure Caleb is doing well and has what he needs supersedes any goals and accomplishments I could ever achieve for myself.

People often ask me what it feels like to have a Ph.D. They marvel at the fact that I was able to complete a task that only 1% of the World's population is able to accomplish. While I am pleased with my achievement, I am even more humbled by it. When I was going through the grueling tasks of doing my statistical analysis and finishing up the final two chapters of my Dissertation, I considered the magnitude of my success and how much I had overcome to get to the finish line. And while I was so proud of myself for having done such a great feat, raising My Caleb forced me to remain grounded, to not become high-minded, and to keep things in their proper perspective.

No matter what letters were behind my name, simply receiving a phone call from Caleb's school saying he was having a bad day, always served as a reminder that there are some things, I cannot control nor conquer. I can only try to make them better. It's interesting how you can simultaneously feel like you are on top of the world in one area and in the lowest valley in another.

Like any other parent, I want nothing but the very best for My Caleb that life has to offer. I recognize that while working within the confines of his Autism Diagnosis, my options are limited. I dislike the fact that this Autism Diagnosis and Speech Impairment, has so much influence in the way that Caleb's life is lived. He deserves a fighting chance just like any other Mainstream Child to make his mark on this world and to have a great life. The rules of Autism, however, want to restrict or end those chances altogether.

It will always be my life's quest to find the right *"formula"* for Caleb – a specifically designed method of learning and communicating where he can make his wants and needs known. Finding this "formula" is what drives me. It's what gives me the strength to get up from those moments of tears and fatigue, to keep walking and moving forward, until I find that right combination for Caleb.

I recognize the great responsibility I have been given in obtaining my Ph.D. It is not just for me to enjoy, but rather to use it as an avenue to bring about more awareness to the difficulties Caleb and children with

Special Needs and their Families face every day. It allows me to bring more awareness to the unique services our children and families need. This degree gives me a greater platform to serve as a Community Activist to speak out against the many injustices our children and community face; and it allows me to fight and demand that our Special Needs Children and Families are represented and considered in all high-level decisions.

Yes, I am excited about being a Ph.D., I am so grateful to have accomplished this momentous task and to have this tremendous honor bestowed upon me. While I did the work to earn it, it was GOD who gave me the grace, the mind, the strength, and the wherewithal to do it, all while raising a young, newly Diagnosed Autistic Child.

The things I face daily while raising Caleb keep me humble and pliable. They keep me close to My GOD. Caleb's Autism Diagnosis always reminds me that no matter how high I go in life, there is a part of me that will always need GOD. For, it is only in HIM that I can find the strength that I need to never give up on my son nor myself.

I will not fail GOD in using my Ph. D. to the fullest and best of my ability! This degree is not about me, but about fulfilling my life's calling and purpose to be a Voice for our Special Needs Community. I will use this degree to bring glory and honor to GOD'S Name and not my own.

DR. RHONDA BROWN-CROWDER

CHAPTER TEN

"OUR PAST PREPARES US FOR OUR FUTURE"

W hether you are a new person to this Special Needs Parenting Journey, or you have been walking it for a while wondering if you will be able to withstand, I can tell you, you are well-able! While the Journey seems arduous, sometimes overwhelming, and often unending, please let me reassure you that you have what it takes to endure and to overcome. Like me, I'm sure if you look back over the course of your life, you will see you had nuggets of time and experiences that prepared you then to be able to raise this Special Needs Child now.

One of the most life-defining events for me was, while growing up and for most of my life, I always felt like a misfit and out of place. I always felt like a square peg trying desperately to fit into a round hole. And no matter how hard I tried to fit in and to be the person I thought everyone wanted me to be, I could never fully accomplish it. I got close to it sometimes, but inevitably I would always find myself reverting to being, as many called me, a *'weird'* child. I always felt like in order to receive the love, acceptance, and approval of those closest to me, I had to be this person that was completely foreign to me.

My actions were never enough. They wanted my mind to work in a certain way and for me to see the world in a certain way, but no matter how hard I tried, I just couldn't do it. When trying to do so, I always felt like I was going against the very core of who GOD created me to be. By telling me to change and to be different, they were in essence telling me that GOD was wrong, and HE made a mistake when HE created me the way HE did.

How can you ask anyone to be anything other than themselves? I felt invisible and invaluable. I honestly felt like if I no longer existed on this earth, it would not matter, and that no one would even notice. I also felt like I was always searching for a place to belong; searching for a place where I felt like I fit and wasn't the weird person or the odd man out; searching for someone to see value in me; searching for someone to tell me that I mattered, and they approved of me.

Growing up in those early days was a very lonely and painful time for me. For years, I tried to fight those feelings of rejection and not belonging. For years I felt great humiliation and isolation because I was different. I felt like I was being punished and ostracized for something of which I had no control. Even though I knew I had nothing to do with the way GOD created me and how people viewed me, it didn't stop me from feeling ashamed and inadequate. I wanted so desperately to be the way others wanted me to be so that I could feel loved and accepted; but no matter how hard I tried, I always fell short.

For many years, my one question to GOD repeatedly was *'Why?'* Why would HE create me in such a way that people would not accept nor understand me? Why would HE surround me with people who are supposed to love and affirm me but made it clear they would never accept who I am, nor try to understand me?

Why would HE surround me with people who would continually demand that I change and be something other than I am, knowing they are never going to give me their love anyways? And, why, if HIS WORD says, *'He formed me and shaped me, and His Love for me is everlasting,'* would HE allow anyone to treat me this way? It all seemed contradictory and confusing to me.

One day, after seemingly asking GOD these questions for a thousand times, I received a sudden revelation. There was an event where our local elementary schools were having different people from the community come in and read to the students. A friend of mine reached out to me and said all the classes at one school had guest readers except one: a Special Education class. She asked me if I was available to come and read. Of course, I said 'Yes!'

In that moment, suddenly, all those feelings I felt while growing up came back like a huge wave. I was at once transformed back in time to being a little girl who was a misfit, who felt devalued and unimportant, and as someone who didn't matter. I thought about our Special Needs

Students and how many of those in our society don't even deem them relevant enough to even be considered for something as simple as reading to them. Just the mere thought of it made me cry gut-wrenching tears. It hurt me to my core. I felt deep anger. Why does society get to decide who deserves value and who doesn't? Why should they get to choose who is worthy of attention and who is not?

The saddest part of all of this for me was the fact that many of our Special Needs Children don't even know they are being excluded, and they are viewed by some as unworthy and unimportant. They don't know, but I know! It became clear to me that I must be their voice. I must speak up on their behalf and let society know that their disregard for and mistreatment of our Special Needs Children is not acceptable.

After reading at the school, I cried on my drive home. Just seeing the students' faces and seeing their excitement from having someone come in and read to them was worth all the money in the world. It filled my heart with such Joy! I suddenly realized, all the feelings of rejection, ridicule, isolation, and exclusion I felt while growing up, enabled me to have a greater level of compassion and understanding for those who are different.

While it was painful growing up feeling the way that I did, and I wished things could have happened differently, I realized I would not have the same heart of compassion, if not for those experiences. Ironically, the deeply painful childhood memories and hurtful feelings I tried so hard to distance myself from, are the very things that are now serving a greater purpose in my life. Those experiences allow me to now feel the hurting heart our Special Needs Children cannot express; the deep anguish they carry inside; the weight of the burdens they bear each day; and their unending search to find a place where they belong and are accepted simply for who they are.

My life's experiences and raising Caleb has shown me that GOD can take all our heartache, pain and disappointments and use them to strengthen and equip us as we walk in our purpose. The things I was always told were 'flaws' in my personality are the things I now need to raise My Caleb and be the best mother for him. I can now fully appreciate these 'flaws' and see beauty in them. My weirdness, creativity, high energy, wackiness, child-like-enthusiasm, and marching to the beat of a different drum is exactly what Caleb needs!

As a child, I also felt like I was filled to the brim with unrequited love. I was so desperate to give it to those who were supposed to love and affirm me, and to receive it as well. I carried the weight of that love inside me into adulthood. When GOD gave me Caleb, HE gave me someone HE knew would need every ounce of that love and affirmation to grow and to prosper. HE gave me someone that I can pour all of my heart and love into, and he never tires of receiving it. HE gave me someone who loves me unconditionally for all that I am and thinks there is no one greater. HE filled that void in me that said I was never good enough. Had I not grown up feeling void and misplaced, I might not have appreciated the vast love that Caleb needs, and I now have the capacity to give.

Like me, I'm sure there are things that others didn't value in you that are now serving you well as you raise your Special Needs Child. Always remember, nothing we go through in this life is ever in vain nor wasted. Every bit of your trials and challenges, including the pain, are important and they serve a higher purpose.

If you are dealing with a difficult time right now and are feeling lost, inadequate, and ill-equipped, I am here to tell you firsthand that *'All things will work together for your good,'* as the Bible says. In time, they will serve a purpose in your and your child's life, and it is going to be meaningful and impactful.

CHAPTER ELEVEN
"WHOSE REPORT WILL YOU BELIEVE?"

A s you continue on this Autism and Special Needs Journey, you will find yourself confronted with many conflicting scenarios. There will be numerous ARDs and IEP documents, evaluations, and pages and pages of documentation throughout your child's Educational Journey telling you all the things they cannot do. In those moments, there are no ways of escape as you have your child's Diagnosis staring you glaringly in the face.

While I have seen these reports many times throughout the years, you can never be fully prepared to see 35 pages of words describing your child in a way that you know is not entirely who they are. I am in no way weak nor a wimp, but my first reaction when confronted with these reports always makes me feel overwhelmed and moved to tears.

You can't imagine what it feels like to have someone tell you that your child cannot, and most likely will never be able to do the things that we consider 'normal' in our society. There's a great sadness that comes with the thought that this might be the way your child has to live the rest of their life. There's a sadness that society is in essence saying, your child is not good enough. There is a sadness that your child will be judged by others as being inadequate and unimportant. There is a sadness that cuts you deep to the core; it grabs ahold of your heart and wraps itself around it, not wanting to let go. It makes you feel like you are utterly defeated before you ever even start.

At some point, I must just stop reading the report and put it down. I know if I don't, my head and my heart will be filled with all the negative things, and I won't be able to see clearly any of the positive. In situations like this, I am reminded of that scripture that asks, *'Whose report will you believe?"* On one hand I have this 35-page report from all the experts in their fields, who are fully licensed and trained in their respective areas in essence saying, unless some miracle occurs, Caleb's future is bleak. On the other hand, I have the Bible and my faith that tells me *'With GOD all things are possible.'*

It is not a matter of my questioning those who have evaluated Caleb, and even their Diagnosis. I am intelligent enough to know that there are clearly some learning and developmental issues going on with him that need to be addressed. And I am continually working with each of the 'experts' to make sure that Caleb is getting all the help he needs. These are things I do in the natural, based on their reports.

In the spiritual, however, I choose to believe GOD's Report. As I am working in the natural, my heart and my faith are rooted and grounded in the spiritual. My faith and the Bible tell me that as I am getting Caleb the help and services he needs, *'In a moment, in the twinkling of an eye,'* his heart, mind, and mouth can miraculously align, and he can be one of those persons who overcame their Autism Diagnosis to do great things. I firmly believe this miracle is going to one day happen for My Caleb. I choose to believe the Report of the Lord that tells me, *'All things are possible.'*

I wish I could tell you that I always stand firm in my faith, and that I never waiver in my belief that GOD is going to help Caleb overcome his challenges. Unfortunately, that is not always the case. I grew up in church, and I am a Woman of Faith. To overcome my childhood and accomplish the things that I have, I had to have a strong faith. I would be dishonest, however, if I said raising a child with Special Needs does not challenge my faith daily. I'm not proud to admit that my emotions go back and forth between faith and fear when it comes to Caleb and his future. I know GOD understands that I am human and am not perfect, and that is why I need HIS Strength every day.

Even while standing in faith that GOD is going to take care of My Caleb, I still deal with that underlying fear that something is going to happen to him, and I won't be there to help him. As I said previously, on one hand I have hope that My Caleb will one day be a 'miracle' cases you read about and will either be able to overcome his Autism and Special Needs, or he will learn to live a wholly independent life while dealing with them. And yet I deal with the fear that he won't be able to overcome them;

that he'll continue getting older; and he won't be able to take care of himself once I'm gone.

It's a constant battle. The good that comes from the battle, however, is that it keeps me continually in the presence of My Lord. If I had no other reason to pray while in this life, this is it! I realize the stakes are too high for me to not be serious about My Caleb's upbringing and future. I can't afford to fail. And so, I find myself going time and time again to THE ONE I know who has all the answers. I go to HIM not only for wisdom and a better understanding of how to raise Caleb, but for me as well.

For the times when I feel helpless, tired, overwhelmed, and as if I am fighting a never-ending battle making no progress, HE is THE ONE who strengthens me, renews me, and encourages me. HE gives me the fortitude I need to keep going. HE is THE ONE who reminds me of the 'prize' I am fighting for: My Dear Son Caleb!

When we are confronted with the issues of life, we must decide how we will answer the question: *'Whose report will you believe?'* Are we going to believe all the negative things that are going on around us, telling us that things are never going to get better and will always remain the same?

Or are we going to believe the Bible and the REPORT OF THE LORD that tells us:

➢ *All things are possible*

➢ *Those who place their hope in HIM will never be made ashamed*

➢ *HIS Strength is made perfect in our weakness*

➢ *HE will never leave us nor forsake us*

➢ *All things (even the seemingly bad and unexplained) are working together for our go*

ALL ROADS LEAD TO LOVE

As you are confronted with life's issues, *Whose Report Will You Believe?* How will you choose to live your life? Will you choose to live in despair and defeat, or with optimism and hope? It is a question that we must answer daily. If we choose to believe GOD'S REPORT, HE has promised to give us the strength we need to deal with all of life's situations. HE tells us that when we are in our lowest and weakest state, it is HIS strength not ours, that will bring us through.

CHAPTER TWELVE
"HOPE IS HARD TO KILL"

The daily pressures of raising a child with Special Needs can sometimes be unimaginable. I think most of us would agree that we could deal with just about anything if we knew it wasn't going to last. When raising a child with Special Needs, it sometimes feels like you are running an unending marathon. With every step you take, you are hopeful that it will lead you closer to a finish line that you cannot see. A part of you wants to quit so many times, but you know the costs are too high. If you quit, who's going to do those things that are necessary for your child? Who else can he or she always count on, but you? What happens to them if you let them down?

You can't even afford to let your guard down for one moment. Because of that pressure, you often feel like you are living in a place between heartbreak and hope – feeling worn out, fatigued, and wanting to quit; and yet you are still taking one more step with hope in your heart. You hope that today will be the day that things change, and your child will receive a developmental breakthrough.

It is a very lonely place to be in at times. It's hard to admit, even to those who love and accept us the most, that we are tired, weak, and overwhelmed - especially when it comes to caring for our Special Needs Children. We don't want people to judge us and think we are bad parents. We don't want them to think that we are uncaring and are not always giving our children our very best. We don't want them to think that even for a minute we are not hopeful about their future.

Many times, the internal battles we fight are not about having Faith, but more about having Trust, while maintaining our Hope. *Faith* says you believe whatever you are hoping for can happen, and GOD can do whatever it is you are asking for HIM to do for your child. *Trust* says you believe HE will do it for You. And, *Hope*, is what keeps you going until the things you are waiting for come to pass.

While hope sometimes seems frail, it is hard to kill. Hope is stubborn. It's relentless. It's dogmatic. Once you allow hope to take root in your heart, it won't let you go. So many times, when dealing with difficult situations with Caleb, I became so fed up, I decided I wasn't going to hope anymore. I wasn't going to expect any changes. I was giving up. I wasn't going to fight. While I went to bed in that state of mind, I still found myself waking up the next morning with a little sliver of hope, telling me *'Today just might be the day that things change for Caleb.'*

There are times when I think raising My Caleb is the very best thing that has ever happened to me, and that I can do it all; and then there are times when I collapse onto the floor in a heap, with tears pouring down my face, asking GOD to give me the strength to take care of Caleb and not let me fail. And then I ask myself how can I tell you, the reader, to keep going when I feel like a fumbling bumbling mess myself? How can I tell you to hold on when I feel like letting go? I can tell you this because I know the Grace of GOD that continues to flow through me and gives me the strength to overcome, will flow through you as well. HE will enable you to continue the Journey.

Oftentimes, when I am dealing with life's challenges, it's not so much that I desire for the situation to change, but more that I need to know that GOD is watching, and HE is proud of how I am carrying the tremendous load HE has placed upon my shoulders. No matter who we are or how strong we are, we all need that reassurance from our HEAVENLY FATHER. One nod from HIM; one word of encouragement; one pat on the back, or one thumbs up, can give us the strength and fuel we need to fight 10,000 more battles. It is during those times when I feel the most desperate to hear from HIM, HE sends someone unexpectedly with a word of encouragement to say:

o *You are a great Mom!*

o *You are a strong Mom!*

o *Caleb is so blessed to have you fighting for him!*

o *I admire the way you never give up!*

o *You and Caleb are an Inspiration to me!*

o   *Thank You for Advocating for our Special Needs Children and Community!*

Even during the times when it seems like GOD has completely left us and is forcing us to deal with life's challenges on our own, HE is still with us, orchestrating every moment of our lives. HE uses the words of others at the exact right time to give us the strength we need to continue standing, hoping, praying, and waiting for a change to come.

When the words come, the people who speak to them often have no idea what is going on in our lives at that moment. It is GOD'S way of letting us know HE sees us, and HE is still working behind the scenes on our behalf. These people have no idea how close we are to the breaking point. They don't know, but Our HEAVENLY FATHER knows; and HE uses their mouths to be a source to speak new strength, hope, and blessings into our spirits.

Yes, there are enormous challenges I face every day to navigate Caleb safely through life, his daily routines, and this Autism Journey. I often feel so tired and worn out that I can't take another step. And then, I take one look into his big, beautiful, brown eyes, and I see his big smile, and it just melts my heart. And then suddenly, I find myself wiping the tears from my eyes, picking myself up, dusting myself off, and pledging to keep fighting for him. I am reminded that I can never quit because Caleb is depending on me.

CHAPTER THIRTEEN

"IT'S ALL ABOUT HIM"

When GOD gives us challenges that seem insurmountable on this Autism and Special Needs Journey, it might feel like HE is trying to 'kill' us or is waiting to see just how much weight it will take to make us fall apart. We may spend a lot of time praying asking GOD to change our situations and make them better, not realizing the situations are changing us for the better. Yes, I want My Caleb to improve in his development to the point where he can function and thrive in Mainstream Society and live a full and independent life. I pray continually for that to happen. Meanwhile, I recognize how GOD is continually giving me the necessary tools and extra measures of Grace to function successfully throughout the day to make sure all the many things I need to do for him get done.

Caleb's Autism Diagnosis completely changed my mind and the idea of success. The feelings I get from contributing to the success of others, helping them realize their dreams, and making them feel loved and valued, is a feeling greater than anything I could have ever felt from achieving my own accomplishments. Caleb's Autism Diagnosis changed my perspective on life so much. Putting myself first, and meeting my goals and desires, is something I can no longer imagine doing. I am here on this earth to live for the betterment of Caleb and others, and to be a blessing to them.

Your Special Needs Journey and challenges may be tough but know that GOD will give you the "tools" that are necessary for you to fight and to keep moving forward. HE will be with you until such a time HE has designed for your situation to come to an end. Like me, you may be hopeful that your child's Special Needs situation will one day end, but maybe it won't? Or maybe it won't end in the way you hoped expected. We must learn to recognize the priceless revelations we gain during the challenges we face, that we wouldn't have gained otherwise. These challenges are the things that GOD uses to make us better people. They are the things HE uses to make us stronger so we can reach out to help others who are struggling and wondering how they are going to make it through.

At the end of the day, our lives are all about HIM. HE is our Creator. HE is the Potter; we are the Clay. No matter what we are confronted with: children's' issues, financial issues, health issues, mental issues, emotional issues, or interpersonal issues, they are all designed for us to go through them and use them to Glorify GOD. It's all about bringing Glory to HIM!

One day, I was having a really hard time. I was feeling low and defeated. Autism was winning. My Tears filled my face. Dear Dad had passed away a few years prior, and I was missing him terribly. He always had a way of talking to me and calming me down when I started feeling

hopeless and overwhelmed. He loved Caleb immensely and was such a proud 'Big Daddy!' He always told me he believed Caleb would one

day be talking so much I would have to tell him to be quiet, and that he was going to do great things. He and Caleb were both lefties and loved chocolate milk. One of Caleb's middle names carries on his 'Brown' name.

As I was sitting, lamenting in despair, I happened to look up, and noticed a gift he had given me for Mother's Day a few years ago. It was a decorative plaque with beautiful words from a child to their mother. When he gave it to me, Dad said since Caleb couldn't tell me himself how he felt about me, the words in the poem represented the things he would say if he could.

The plaque talked about how the child realized 'he' and his mother were brought together for a reason, and how having her love will cause him to grow to his fullest potential. 'He' thanked her for loving him even after seeing him at his worst. 'He' said he was grateful for their everlasting special bond and thanked her for being his guide.

When I read the words on the plaque I cried like a baby. Not only did it bless me immensely as I read the words 'from' Caleb to me, but it also blessed me because it was like my Dad was letting me know in that moment that he was still with me and everything was going to be okay.

I believe these are exactly the words our Autism and Special Needs Children, who are not able to verbally express how they feel, would say to their moms, dads, grandparents, and other caregivers that are raising them. Reading those words brought such comfort and peace to my heart. It gave me the strength I needed to wipe my face, dry my eyes, and to continue fighting for Caleb, for another day.

CHAPTER FOURTEEN
"A KEEN AWARENESS OF THE MOMENT"

I have always been a future-focused person. While I strive to enjoy the present, and learn from the past, I find myself always looking towards the future – towards the things to come. I set short- and long-term goals based on this concept. Doing so allows me to always have something to work towards. This mindset keeps me moving forward and serves as a motivating force to keep me working hard and maintaining my hope.

After I had Caleb, and he began to grow and develop, my natural path of thought was always towards his future. Before his Autism Diagnosis he was progressing well. I already had it set in my mind the goals I wanted him to accomplish in life. I could see myself crossing them off my list one-by-one, while he moved seamlessly from one milestone to the next.

At the point of Caleb's Autism Diagnosis, his development had come to a complete stop. I had no idea how to process that change. It went against everything I had planned and imagined for his life. If he had not been diagnosed with Autism, I would have just expected him to keep accomplishing things. I have very high expectations for myself, and I was on the pathway of having the same for him as well. I'm sure that as he met those accomplishments, rather than stopping to really celebrate them, I would have given him a pat on the back or a high five and said, *"Okay, Caleb! Let's go higher! Let's do better!"*

Having My Caleb and dealing with his Autism Diagnosis changed my life completely. It forced me to re-evaluate the things I desired for him and to set more realistic expectations for his accomplishments. His Diagnosis not only made me a better person, but a completely different person. Rather than waiting for him to do something 'grand' to celebrate him and his success, I now find little things to celebrate that I likely would have overlooked of quietly dismissed. Now, I have come to deeply love, appreciate, and rejoice in those moments of success and to treasure them.

I now have such a greater sense of awareness of the passing of time, and the importance of enjoying every single moment. Because of Caleb, my view of life is multi-dimensional. When I am experiencing even the simplest occurrences with him, I am so keenly aware of the fact that I am living presently in that dimension and moment, that will one day be a great memory.

And along with the joy and exuberance of that moment, I am also experiencing another dimension of underlying sadness. The sadness comes from knowing that even as I am experiencing that moment in my present, it is simultaneously becoming a part of my past. And while I want it to last forever, it is fleeting and moving, right before my eyes. I want to hold on to it, but I can't. I must let it go. Once that moment is gone, it can never be relived again. Yes, there will be many more moments, but never that one moment.

Because of this greater sense of awareness, I now pay more attention to the colors, the sounds, the laughter, and even the tears, and everything happening around me; knowing that one day, as I look back on them, these moments will bring joy to my age-weary soul. I now allow myself to soak up every detail. I am constantly reminded that even if we live to be 100 years old, it will never be enough time to spend with our Special Needs Children and the ones we love.

I now have a heightened sense of awareness of the magnitude of life and even death. My awareness of death is not in a morbid sense, or necessarily in a sad sense, but just a greater awareness of its inevitability. So, I now pay more attention to life's smallest details: The sound of Caleb's giggles when I tickle him; the way he likes to close his eyes and feel the wind on his face when we are driving in the car with the windows down; the feel of his little hands on my face when he takes my face into his hands and pulls me close to give me Eskimo kisses; the way his dimple appears in his left cheek when he squeezes his eyes closed with excitement, the cleft in his chin, and the way his lips pucker when he cries. I've learned to notice every detail.

Caleb's Autism Diagnosis gave me an unexpected gift. The moments I just described would have been lost to me had he not been Diagnosed. I likely would have been so focused on moving him from one success to another, I wouldn't have ever stopped to fully recognize and then celebrate those moments. Because of Caleb, I now fully understand how precious life is and what a wonderful gift it is to not only live it but to share it with those you love and hold dear.

I am now more aware of how important it is to not waste time dwelling on things that people did or didn't do; promises that were broken; the times people disappointed me and let me down; and the hurtful things that were said. I have learned to live life with less expectations of people and to let them off the hook more quickly. I have come to understand that as my life is difficult and challenging at times, others' lives are as well. And when they make mistakes, I have learned to give them the benefit of the doubt of just having a bad day.

I no longer spend my precious time trying to always figure things out or to move from one moment to the next. I've learned to slow life down a bit. In the past, I would have been running full speed in the mornings trying to get Caleb and I dressed and out the door. Now, on occasion, I'll stop to take a moment to lie right next to him, to look him in the eyes, nose to nose, and wish him a Good Morning and let him know he is my Cutie Pie.

I'll tell him to *"Wakey Up!"* And then, he'll give me a big sleepy smile, and throw his arm around my neck and pull me close and lay his lips on my cheek as an act of giving me a kiss. He hasn't figured out the "smack" part yet that goes with it, but I know it is his special kiss.

I'll tell him how much I love him and how he's going to have a great day. I'll stay right there with him in that moment for a few minutes

– all the while ignoring that voice in my head that keeps telling me I better hurry up or we'll be late. In the past, I would've listened to that voice and missed that beautiful moment with Caleb. Now, I've learned to stop and have these experiences, which leave me with sweet memories I can treasure forever.

Having Caleb has taught me it is so important to let people know that they matter to you. It's one thing to say you love them, which is something they can always hear in their minds, but it's an even greater thing to share a moment with them and give them a memory they can later enjoy repeatedly in their hearts.

I've learned, no matter how many things you accomplish in this world, there is no greater feeling than having someone count on you for something, and then for you to come through for them. Even if they are just counting on you to share a smile or a listening ear, to make them a meal, or to make sure they are properly clothed, you are the one they are looking to, to get what they need. Having that level of responsibility, and then seeing it through to the end, makes you feel like the most special person in the world. Caleb counts on me every day, and I do everything within my power not to let him down.

Only GOD knows how much time I will have in this world with My Caleb. So, with every baseball game; track meet; school picnic, field day and holiday function; with every speech, occupational therapy, and music session; with all things present and with all the things to come, I will not only be present in that moment with Caleb, but I will live in that moment. I will experience all that it has to offer, knowing that from one second to the next, it is moving from my present into my past; and is becoming a distant memory of my future, never to be lived again.

I have found the Journey and Roads of Autism are filled with many amazing gifts, wrapped up in irrefutable challenges, waiting to be overcome, so their gloriousness can be revealed.

CHAPTER FIFTEEN
"ALL ROADS LEAD TO LOVE"

I f I were to reduce the content of this entire book down to a few words to explain all that our Autism and Special Needs Journey entails, it would read like this…

DR. RHONDA BROWN-CROWDER

"All Roads Lead to Love"

All Roads Lead to Love
Those zealous and strong,
some strewn with pain and heartache
as you're moving along.

All Roads Lead to Love
The good ones and the bad,
the happy, crazy, ecstatic ones
and the ones that are sad.

All Roads Lead to Love
With times of excitement and joy,
times of heartbreak and disappointments
hurling us to the floor.

All Roads Lead to Love
With days of light and the dark,
days you know everything, then nothing
and have completely missed the mark.

ALL ROADS LEAD TO LOVE

All Roads Lead to Love

With rough terrain and familiar paths,

days of triumphant victories

and defeats that stir up wrath.

All Roads Lead to Love

No matter life's contradictions nor pace,

because the person walking with you

is your reason for staying in the race.

All Roads Lead to Love

Take a moment to look aside,

at the Person sharing this Journey with you

for Whom Your Love You Cannot Hide.

Written by Dr. Rhonda Brown-Crowder,

Inspired by the Holy Spirit.

May 25, 2022, at 7:30 p.m.

As you finish reading this book, I pray you have been bettered, strengthened, enlightened, and encouraged. I hope you have found some nuggets of wisdom and strategies to carry with you, as you and your Special Needs Child continue to navigate through the untraveled Roads, Life's Journey has in store.